Etsy Business Launch:

The Complete Guide to Making
Six Figures Selling on Etsy

Alyssa Garner and Garrett Garner

Disclaimer

Note from the authors: Below is the standard disclaimer that books like this typically include. To summarize in our own words, we would like you to know that starting or running a business of any kind comes with inherent risk. If you choose to take the leap, you alone are responsible for the actions and choices you make in your business. While we wish you all the success in the world, we can't make any guarantees that the steps outlined here will have any particular outcome for you, as results are based on many factors. Always consider your decisions carefully, while also maintaining a healthy dose of optimism!

The information in this book is for informational and educational purposes only. It should not be construed as business, tax, or legal advice of any kind. All information and resources found in this book are based on the opinions of the authors alone unless otherwise noted.

The authors of this book assume no responsibility or liability for any consequence resulting directly or indirectly from any action or inaction you take based on the information found in this book.

While the authors have made every effort to provide accurate information at the time of publication, they do not assume any responsibility for errors or changes that occur after publication.

This book is intended to be used only as a general guide, and not as a sole source of information on the subject matter. Always consult a licensed professional before attempting any techniques outlined in this book.

Congrats!

Congratulations on picking up this book! You currently hold in your hands the keys to successfully launching your very own Etsy business.

We're SO excited to hear what you think! Once you've finished the book, we would love it if you'd leave an honest review on Amazon.

You can do this by searching for the book title on Amazon.com, scrolling to "Customer Reviews" at the bottom of the page, and clicking "Write a customer review" to the left of the screen.

Your review provides valuable feedback and helps us bring more books and resources to you. We appreciate your support!

Contents

Introduction

Imagine this. You wake up each day to a business that's entirely yours: the six-figure Etsy shop of your dreams.

You don't have to answer to demanding bosses, unrealistic deadlines, or obnoxious coworkers. Instead, you're free to just create and allow true passion to flow through your work.

You wake up when you want to and work on your own schedule. You have the flexibility to take vacations, spend time with loved ones, and relax with self-care, all while being the CEO of your very own thriving Etsy business.

Your Etsy shop represents who you are and what you love to do, while also making you an income that far exceeds that of your nine-to-five job. You're able to create, do, and afford more than you ever thought possible.

You make a six-figure income selling your unique crafts to loyal customers who love your shop and are excited to buy from you. The five-star reviews are flying in and your customer base is growing every day. At a certain point, sales become effortless and repeat buyers are the norm.

You no longer look enviously at other successful shop owners wondering, "How do they do it?" because you're now armed with all the secrets needed to skyrocket your own Etsy business right to the top.

You feel confident in who you are and are excited about what the future holds. You're no longer afraid to put yourself out there.

You're the proud owner of a six-figure Etsy business and your shop just keeps expanding from there. You've truly made it.

If any part of the scenario above sounds exciting to you, then you've come to the right place! This book in your hands is designed to help you achieve all of the above and SO much more. The ultimate six (or even seven) figure Etsy shop that you've always dreamed of is now well within your reach.

Whether you're looking for your Etsy business to be a profitable side hustle that generates extra cash or a full-time income that exceeds your current nine-to-five, this book has all the must-have secrets, tips, and strategies you'll need to get there.

Maybe you're brand new to Etsy and starting from the ground floor. Or maybe, you already have an Etsy shop but find yourself frustrated by how little money you earn for your time. Regardless of where you're starting from, you CAN launch, grow, and scale a successful Etsy business in less time than you can imagine.

This book isn't just another basic tutorial on how to start your Etsy shop but rather a powerful guide on how to actually make money on Etsy. Lots of money.

We'll provide the exact step-by-step formula for building a successful Etsy business that rewards your time and dedication through a loyal customer base, an expanding Etsy presence, and a steadily growing income.

If you're reading this, you've already taken the very first step.

Who This Book Is For

This book is the definitive guide to all things Etsy and is designed to help anyone turn their shop into a thriving six-figure business (even if you don't have a shop yet!).

This book is for:

- Those who are brand new to Etsy and want all the tools necessary to create a flourishing business from the start
- Those who already have an Etsy shop and want expert guidance on making consistent sales, popularizing their brand, and growing their income
- Those who already have a successful Etsy shop and want an effective strategy for taking their business to the next level (aka six figures and beyond!)

In short, this book can help ANYONE in any stage of their Etsy journey achieve the six-figure shop of their dreams. It just takes work, dedication, and mastery of all the necessary steps.

This book covers all the bases of a six-figure Etsy business from the fundamentals all the way up to advanced strategies. Even if you already own a successful Etsy shop, we highly recommend that you go through each step in order, resisting the urge to jump ahead to the advanced strategies.

In our experience, the businesses that never reach their full potential are typically the ones that are lacking in the fundamentals. It's important to start with a strong foundation, so you can easily catapult to six figures later on. You need to build the launchpad first, in order to skyrocket.

How This Book Is Different

If you're reading this book, chances are, this isn't the first Etsy book or resource you've ever picked up. Unfortunately, it's not uncommon for business-related books, articles, and courses to overpromise and underdeliver, leaving you disappointed or confused.

So what makes this book different?

- This book is based on our signature six-step framework for Etsy success. We go through each step in order, so you'll never be lost or confused. This framework is unique to our book and can't be found anywhere else.
- This book contains all you need to successfully launch your Etsy business and nothing you don't. No fluff—just straightforward strategy that works.
- This book explores every aspect of running a successful Etsy business. In addition to in-depth Etsy strategy, you'll also learn key business principles, mindset hacks, troubleshooting tips, and more. We'll make sure you're completely covered, no matter what.
- This book is complete and self-contained. Unlike many business books, ours isn't designed to upsell you an expensive course or mastermind group. Our entire strategy for Etsy success is right here in your hands.
- This book is written by two entrepreneurs with almost a decade of experience running multiple businesses (more about us later!).

How This Book Works

Every successful business starts with an effective framework. We call ours "The Six-Figure Etsy Blueprint."

Our goal is to show you the quickest and easiest path to six figures on Etsy. No stress or drama—just results.

In order to achieve this, we've created a powerful six-step curriculum that covers all aspects of launching a $100,000+ Etsy business:

Step 1: Start
Step 2: Launch
Step 3: Optimize
Step 4: Grow
Step 5: Scale
Step 6: Skyrocket

The rest of this book covers each of the concepts above in complete detail, including all the actionable steps needed to move forward to the next stage.

We suggest reading through the entire book FIRST before implementing the steps. Once you understand the full framework, you can go over it a second time and begin taking action.

Remember to follow the blueprint in order, resisting the urge to jump ahead. The first three steps are, in many ways, the most important because they are the basis for your six-figure business.

Once you've read through the book, commit to learning the framework and putting it into practice each day. Always remember that action plus consistency equals results!

Overview: The Six-Figure Etsy Blueprint

Before we get started, here's a quick rundown of the six steps, so you know what to expect. Each step builds on the previous ones helping you create a successful Etsy business from the ground up.

Step One: Start

In this section, we'll cover all the essentials of a six-figure shop, including niche, market research, products, branding, and ideal customer base.

You'll learn the key strategies that make the difference between a shop that succeeds and one that doesn't. Once these elements are in place, you'll have the groundwork needed to grow and scale to $100,000 and beyond.

By nailing this step, you're nearly guaranteed to have a profitable and high-performing shop.

Step Two: Launch

In this section, you'll learn how to set up and convert your Etsy shop into a sales machine that generates immediate income. We'll cover how to open your shop, create listings that sell, price your products, and fulfill orders like a pro.

In order to grow and scale your shop, you'll need a professional presence and enticing listings. You'll learn the eye-opening secrets to mastering the Etsy algorithm, taking gorgeous product photos, and choosing profitable keywords that will sell your items like hotcakes.

We'll share the ideal pricing formula that maximizes both sales and profit margins, along with the must-know strategies that ensure products are shipped quickly and safely, while also saving you time and money in the process.

Step Three: Optimize

In this step, we'll cover optimization strategies that will supercharge your shop to the best that it can be. You'll learn how to provide excellent customer service that leads to five-star reviews, positive word of mouth, repeat customers, and increased sales.

We'll share our simple process for receiving a constant influx of glowing reviews on autopilot from happy customers. We'll also address how to deal with the occasional difficult customer or negative review in a productive way.

By properly launching and optimizing your shop, you'll be certain that your business is set up for optimal success, when it's time to grow in the next step.

Step Four: Grow

In this step, we'll share the highly coveted marketing secrets of a six-figure Etsy business.

We'll teach you the powerful marketing principles that will ensure you succeed in any business, as well as the social media framework that results in massive sales. You'll also learn how to grow your email list, connect with your subscribers, and write powerful emails that sell (without sounding "salesy").

We'll explore paid advertising and how to receive the greatest bang for your buck, alongside powerful growth strategies to triple your sales for free with almost no effort.

Our marketing strategies are uniquely designed to skyrocket your income in the shortest amount of time, while also staying true to your brand and who you are (you'll never feel slimy or icky!).

Step Five: Scale

You're already on track to build a six-figure business. In this step, we'll make it official!

You'll learn all the ins and outs of running a professional business, including setting up an LLC, tackling taxes and accounting, choosing a mission statement, creating business cards, and establishing an online business presence.

While these concepts can sound intimidating, we'll break down each task in a way that's easy to understand and effortless to apply, so you can keep building your business without missing a beat.

We'll also cover outsourcing, which allows your business to soar to new heights with less work and zero overwhelm.

Step Six: Skyrocket (to $100K and Beyond!)

This is it—you've made it! In this section, you'll step fully into the mindset of a successful business owner, so you can continue to grow with confidence and purpose.

We'll reveal our best six-figure secrets, alongside tips for keeping up the momentum. You'll also learn how to diversify your Etsy shop by creating a passive income stream that allows you to grow your bank account even while you sleep.

With this step, your income potential becomes truly limitless. You simply rinse and repeat until you've reached your goals!

About Us

Before we move on, we'd like to spend a quick moment introducing ourselves.

We're Alyssa and Garrett and we love helping budding entrepreneurs (just like you!) reach their dreams of a six-figure income and financial freedom doing what they love.

Our story: We met in college where we bonded over a shared love of horror movies, Italian food, and beer pong. Garrett wanted to ask Alyssa out right from the get-go, but before he got a chance, she had already set him up with one of her friends (whoops!).

The timing never worked out for us in college, but eventually, Garrett *did* ask Alyssa out and the rest is history. We were married within seven months and got started on our shared dream of building a life and business that was completely ours. This was the start of our entrepreneurial empire.

Although we'd each worked on our own business ventures previously, it was our combined experience and unconditional support of one another that catapulted us to the next level. The journey really is more fun when you're in it together.

Fast forward: Now, we own multiple businesses and make more money than we ever thought possible. More importantly, we live life on our own terms doing what we love the most.

Our passion now lies in teaching others to build their own business empires with confidence and ease. Over nearly a decade of trial and error, we've developed an online business strategy that WORKS.

Now, we're here to teach you. Our in-depth Etsy guide contains the practical steps, rooted in sound business principles, that you'll need to grow your shop to six figures faster than you could ever imagine, even if you're a total beginner.

Just believe in yourself, trust the process, and dive right in! Ready to get started?

STEP ONE: START

Congrats! You've made it to the first step in your Etsy business launch.

This is one of the most critical steps you'll take on the path to six figures, as it sets the foundation for all the other stages to come. Many of the concepts in this section alone can skyrocket your shop from side hustle to six-figure business when applied properly.

If you already have an Etsy shop, don't be afraid to look it at, as it is now, and make any adjustments needed to help you succeed.

Ready, set, START!

CHAPTER 1

The Elements of a Six-Figure Shop

Your Etsy journey starts right here with your niche, products, ideal customer, and brand. These elements are the foundation for your Etsy business and an integral part of the six-figure blueprint.

In order to succeed in any business, you need to start with perfect clarity about your unique brand and who it's designed for.

Are you familiar with the expression "When you speak to everyone, you speak to no one"? A lot of us Etsy shop owners are creatives with a lot of different talents and interests. You might be a superstar at making candles, Adirondack chairs, and crochet patterns. But unless you can find a way to tie all three together so they appeal to the same customer, you're going to have to pick one.

You never want to spread yourself too thin as a business owner. It's always best to pick one ideal customer and focus on creating products and a brand that appeal to them. Your goal is to become known within that customer base for being extremely good at what you do.

Your Niche

It all starts here with your niche.

If you've dabbled in Etsy or any other business venture, you might have heard this term before. It's basically just a fancy word for the segment of the Etsy customer base that's in the market for your specific products.

In 2021, approximately 96.3 million active buyers made a purchase on Etsy. Crazy, right?

Needless to say, that's a huge pie and you absolutely cannot and should not try to appeal to all 96.3 million buyers on Etsy. This is why we niche down.

We choose a niche and then we choose a sub-niche of that niche and we keep going until we find a market segment that's large enough to have a significant customer base, but small enough that we still stand out.

Another popular expression that applies here is "a big fish in a small pond." In terms of the Etsy marketplace as a whole, you are a cute little guppy swimming in the Pacific Ocean. But, if you niche down, you'll be able to stand out as a much larger fish in a small pond that still gets plenty of visitors and attention from a specific audience.

So how do you find your niche? It starts with market research.

Market Research

When picking an Etsy niche, you'll want to consider your own interests, talents, and abilities, as well as what customers on Etsy are already looking to buy.

A six-figure Etsy shop is a balance between passion and profit. You'll want to choose a niche that you're passionate about, while also considering its profitability.

The key here is to take what you already love to do and figure out how to make the most money with it. This is where market research comes in handy.

Here's how it works:

1. Start with 1–2 general categories on Etsy that you have the interest and skill set for.

    You can find categories by exploring the general classifications listed at the top of the Etsy desktop site under the search bar (e.g., "Clothing & Shoes," "Home & Living," etc.).

    As an example, if you hover over "Home & Living," you'll see a dropdown on the left side that includes "Bath & Beauty." If you click on that, you'll see several options, including "Skin Care." "Skin Care" is an example of a category.

    "Skin Care" alone has 183,325 results on Etsy at the time of this writing. This is way too much competition for you to stand out, which is why we niche down even further in the next step.

2. When you click on your chosen category, you'll see examples of products that are already popular in this category. Write down a few that stand out to you and ask yourself *who* these products are for.

    With our skin care example, we can see on the first page that most of the products highlight natural ingredients (such as shea butter or turmeric) and are designed to appeal to women.

3. Next, go into the Etsy search bar and type in your category name (i.e., skin care). You'll notice a dropdown appear with Etsy's suggestions for that search term.

Add simple words after your category, such as "for" or "gifts" to bring up more suggestions. You can also search for some of the products or ingredients you found in step 2. Make note of all relevant suggestions that come up in your search.

Some of the terms we searched for were "skin care," "skin care for," "skin care" [with a space next to it], "skin care lotion," "skin care turmeric," and "skin care shea butter." We found suggestions like "skin care kit," "skin care labels," "skin care for kids," "skin care for oily skin," "turmeric soap," "shea butter perfume," and more.

4. Expand your search to Google and see what suggestions come up there. You can even check Pinterest and Instagram, as well.

   We typed "skin care Etsy" into Google search and found "puppy skin care Etsy," "natural skin care Etsy," "organic skin care Etsy," and much more.

   Between steps 3 and 4, you now have a list of potential niches for your shop.

5. Choose the 3–5 niches from your list that you're most interested in. Then, go back to Etsy and type the first one into the search bar.

   Look at how many search results come up, what's popular or a bestseller within this niche, and how many reviews the shops and products in this niche generally receive.

   The number of search results is the level of competition, while the number of reviews shows the level of demand.

   In step 1, we found that a general category on Etsy like "Skin Care" had 183,325 results, but if we search "Skin Care for Kids" instead, we'll see that it only has 2,701 results. This is far less competition.

One of the top-selling products is a body cream for kids that has 261 reviews for the item and 21,000+ reviews for the shop. The shop's primary focus is natural skin care for kids and it's made over 90,000 sales in this niche. This demonstrates high demand on Etsy for products in the "Skin Care for Kids" niche.

The lower competition paired with significant demand shows that "Skin Care for Kids" would be a profitable niche for your Etsy shop.

Repeat this step for each potential niche on your list and circle the most profitable ones.

6. Consider the products you would sell in each one of these profitable niches. Is the niche broad enough that you can brainstorm at least 50–100 different products you could sell within it?

    Again, the key here is to choose a niche that is narrow enough for you to stand out, but broad enough that you have plenty of room to grow and add new inventory.

    For example, with skin care for kids, you could sell a variety of soaps, lotions, bath bombs, body washes, and a whole lot more. The possibilities for new products within this niche are nearly endless, which is a great sign.

If you're just starting out on Etsy, this research will ensure your idea for a shop is profitable and has the proven potential to build a six-figure empire. It allows you to explore small sections of the Etsy marketplace and evaluate whether or not there is already a strong customer base for that niche. Your aim is to choose a niche in which the demand exceeds the competition.

If you already have an Etsy shop, this research can help you tighten up your niche and increase your profitability. There's no need to overhaul your entire shop or start completely anew (unless you want to!). Just a few simple tweaks to your current niche could skyrocket your income.

You can evaluate the profit potential of your current shop by asking yourself:

1. What is my niche?
2. How many search results are there for my niche? Where do my listings rank within these results?
3. Look at your most popular products. Who do they appeal to most and why?
4. Is it possible to niche down further and capture a more specific audience?

For example, let's say you already have a skin-care shop on Etsy, but sales are intermittent and your shop hasn't grown as quickly as you'd like it to. You currently sell all sorts of skin-care items, but your most successful products are your organic sheet masks. So, why not focus more on those?

This doesn't mean you have to stop selling your other products altogether, but niching down to make sheet masks your focus will help your shop stand out. Now, you're competing with 1,218 other search results, as opposed to the whole skin-care category.

This makes it much easier to capture a specific audience and your shop will quickly become the go-to brand for customers who love organic sheet masks. Instead of spreading yourself too thin by creating lots of skin-care items that don't sell as well, you can now focus your efforts on creating more varieties of your most popular product.

Another option is to niche down from just "skin care" to "organic skin care for women," so you can capture a more specific segment of the market (i.e., women looking for natural skin-care products with organic ingredients).

Regardless of where you're starting from, a six-figure business starts with the right niche that exhibits a balance between profit and passion. Just be sure to pick a niche that you're excited about and have the skills to pull off.

If you've never made jewelry before, don't pick a niche in that category, just because it's profitable. Your niche still needs to align with your unique talents and interests. That's what selling on Etsy is all about.

Sometimes, if the passion and talent are there, you simply need to tweak your ideas a bit in order to hit profitability. For example, let's say you make miniature houses out of rusty nails. As creative as that might be, a brief Etsy and Google search will quickly show you that there isn't much of a market for that.

It's nearly impossible to hit six figures if there's no customer base for your products, so why not adjust your idea to give yourself the best chance at success? Maybe try making miniature houses out of a different material instead. One of the best-selling miniature houses on Etsy is a hobbit house made out of resin. Could you make something similar?

At the end of the day, there are thousands of niches that could make you six figures on Etsy. Once you've proven profitability, simply go with your gut and choose what feels right to you.

Remember, you want to start an Etsy business, so you can follow your passion and make money doing what you love. Don't lose sight of that when choosing your niche.

Products

Niche and products go hand in hand on Etsy. While niche is explored first in this book, you can't fully decide on a niche without knowing which products you're going to sell in your shop.

Remember, a niche is simply the segment of the Etsy marketplace that your shop, brand, and products are designed to appeal to. So, if your niche is "Skin Care for Kids" then your products should appeal to that specific demographic. This could include colorful bubble baths, soaps that are shaped like farm animals, and cotton candy bath bombs.

If you're having trouble deciding on a niche, you can always start with which products you want to sell and work backward. Here are some popular items that are already selling well on Etsy to get your creative juices flowing:

- Stickers
- Journals, notebooks, and planners
- Jewelry
- Home decor
- Posters
- Vintage items
- Toys and baby items
- Sewing and crochet patterns
- T-shirts
- Bags and purses
- Phone cases
- Candles
- Crochet patterns
- Skin care
- Printables

The options are endless, as long as the products you choose comply with Etsy's homemade and vintage guidelines. You can find these by searching "What Can I Sell on Etsy?" in the Etsy Help Center.

A successful Etsy business should have around 100 to 125 listings in its shop that appeal to the same customer base. This provides enough variety for your buyers without overwhelming you as an independent shop owner. But, of course, every shop is different and this is just a ballpark number.

And if 100+ listings sound like a lot to you right now, don't freak out! You'll build these up over time.

Just like with choosing your niche, you'll want to research products for your shop that are already proven to sell well and have a significant customer base. Before you add a new product to your shop, always search for it on Etsy and see if customers are already looking to buy this item. Note how many items on the first page of this search result are bestsellers and how many reviews the top listings have.

The last thing you want to do is spend 20 hours making a new product only to later find out that there's no customer base for it. Do your research first and your shop has a much better shot at being profitable. Plus, it will save you a lot of time and headache later down the line.

Remember, your niche isn't just the products you're selling, but also who they're for. We'll explore your ideal customer in the next section.

Ideal Customer

When it comes to a successful Etsy business, there's nothing more important than understanding your customer base and who you're selling to.

Your ideal customer will be at the heart of countless decisions you'll make throughout running your business, such as branding, products, pricing, social media, and so much more.

As a shop owner, you're providing a product that fulfills a customer's needs, wants, or desires. In other words, your customer has a problem and you're providing the solution.

Is your customer looking for a natural face cream that will nurture her skin without needless chemicals? Or maybe your customer is looking for whimsical outdoor decor that will transform her backyard into a garden sanctuary. Or perhaps your customer is looking for that perfect gift for his son who loves outer space.

The only thing that these very different customers have in common is that they're all searching the Etsy marketplace for an answer to their specific wants or needs. If you have the solution, it's your job as a shop owner to make sure it is prominently displayed when the right person searches for it.

This is where your ideal customer comes in. They are the one person you are trying to reach with your shop and products. This customer belongs to the market segment that you identified previously as your niche.

Remember, when you make products designed for everyone, you're selling to no one. This section is designed to help you really home in on who your shop, products, and brand are for, so you can capture the attention of the customers in your niche and skyrocket your sales.

Over 40% of buyers on Etsy are repeat customers. The more products you sell that appeal to one specific type of customer, the more likely they are to buy from you again.

For this reason, each and every one of the 100+ product listings in your shop should be created with the same ideal customer in mind. You can still sell a large variety of products, as long as they are all geared toward the same type of buyer. In other words, focus your efforts on just one segment of Etsy's customer base and you will be rewarded with consistent sales.

To accomplish this, you need to really understand your ideal customer and bring them to life in your shop. They cannot just be a vague idea in your head. You have to really nail down what makes them tick, what they're searching for, and, most importantly, what makes them hit that buy button.

Here are some questions to ask yourself:

- Who is your ideal customer? Nail down some basics like gender, marital status, kids, income, etc. This can obviously be fluid, but will help solidify the image of your ideal customer in your mind.
- Where does your ideal customer shop (aside from Etsy)? What are some of their favorite shops?
- What social media channels does your ideal customer spend the most time on?
- What blogs or websites does your ideal customer visit?
- What does your ideal customer like to do in their free time?
- What does your ideal customer spend money on (besides the essentials like food and housing)? How much are they willing to spend on these nonessentials?

Take the time to answer these questions fully. Write your answers down in a notebook or Word document and keep them handy. Refer back to them throughout your Etsy journey whenever you add a new product or make major changes to your shop or marketing strategy.

This will help you stay focused on what's most important to you as a shop owner: your ideal customer. You'll be able to drown out the noise of what other Etsy shop owners are doing and focus on what you know best: your niche, your brand, and your customer.

Moreover, if you ever find yourself stuck in the weeds, while making key decisions for your business, just ask yourself, "How can I help my ideal customer?" or "What is my ideal customer searching for?" or "What does my ideal customer want or need right now?"

The foundation of any six-figure business is deeply knowing and understanding what your ideal customer wants and needs, and how to provide it to them through your shop and products. Always keep this in mind and your shop will be successful.

Brand

Every successful business has a distinct brand. Your brand is what distinguishes your shop from others that are selling similar products. It's also a great marketing tool.

Your brand ties your shop name, color palette, font, logo, style, and photos together with your niche, ideal customer, and products to create a unique and marketable identity for your business. We'll talk more about each of these elements in detail later on, but deciding on your brand now will help you maintain consistency between all of these components.

Let's say you sell crocheted blankets, clothing, and stuffed toys in your shop. Your niche is custom and personalized items for babies and toddlers aged newborn to three years old. Your ideal customer is the mom who wants one-of-a-kind handmade items for her baby that can't be found anywhere else. She wants her child to stand out when she takes her to Mommy and Me classes and for all her friends to squeal, "Oh my gosh! Where did you get that adorable romper?"

Think about the kind of branding that this ideal customer would resonate with the most, when searching for baby items like yours. She's not likely to identify with a black spidery font and a spooky logo that looks like it belongs in a haunted house. Instead, she would probably be drawn toward a light pink and blue color palette paired with a cute logo.

Consistency is key when it comes to branding. You don't want soft pinks and blues paired with a creepy font. That sends mixed messages about who your products are for.

You never want your ideal customer to wonder if your shop is right for them. You want them to KNOW that your products are everything they've been looking for, so they hit that buy button without thinking twice.

Branding is the main form of communication between you and your ideal customer. Your goal is to consider what appeals to this type of shopper and then create a consistent and marketable brand that communicates, beyond a shadow of a doubt, that your shop is for them.

So how do we do this? It starts with filling in the blanks of this statement:

I sell _____ for _____, so they can _____.

You can think of this statement as the answer to the question, "What do you do?" or the elevator pitch for your brand.

An example would be "I sell organic skin-care products for women with sensitive skin, so they can feel beautiful without experiencing the side effects of harsh chemicals typically found in traditional skin-care products."

This statement speaks directly to one specific type of customer. It is the basis for your brand. Now, you just need a shop name, logo, and colors that align with this brand and clearly convey who your products are for. We'll explore this more in Step Two.

CHAPTER 2

The #1 Secret to Building an Etsy Empire

Now that we've covered the foundation for your business moving forward, we'd like to share one of the biggest secrets to building a sustainable Etsy empire that rewards you with consistent sales and growing revenue.

In the Etsy world, there's a lot of noise. It's a huge marketplace with almost 100 million buyers and over 4 million sellers. There's room for everyone here, but there's also a ton of distraction: other shops and shop owners, what they're doing, what you could be doing, and so on.

You can easily drive yourself crazy going down a path of trying to do everything at once and losing sight of the big picture. This is why we've dedicated a whole chapter to this simple but powerful success secret. If you nail this one important concept, you will stay the course and never veer off track on your way six-figure Etsy greatness.

So here it is: STAY FOCUSED. Focus on your niche, your ideal customer, and your brand. Have the courage and confidence to let everything else go.

We live in a world of infinite options and constant FOMO. But, it's the shop owners who consistently stick with one niche and wake up each day thinking, "How can I help my ONE ideal customer?" that ultimately succeed.

On Etsy, you'll see thousands of shop owners succeeding in lots of different niches. It's sometimes easy to get distracted by shiny objects and consider jumping ship into something new—a new niche, a brand-new shop, maybe even a totally different business venture.

The secret to success on Etsy, and in any business, for that matter, is simple. The ones who stick with it the longest end up making the most money. If you give up after three months, you'll never have the potential to make six figures.

Focus and commitment are the key. Once you have a strong niche and a proven concept that you're excited about, all you really need to succeed is the drive to stick with it and keep pushing forward.

You should, of course, make occasional changes or adjustments to your shop to help it grow stronger. However, making sensible tweaks to your business isn't the same as abandoning it for the next new thing. You're still staying the course, while also have the foresight to adjust what's not working.

As we mentioned earlier, we're usually the creative and talented types here on Etsy. We excel in a lot of different areas and it's easy to get pulled into what everyone else is doing. While you can, of course, look at other similar shops for inspiration, you should never let what others are doing distract you from your goals.

In the coming chapters of this book, you'll find a lot of information about keywords, reviews, social media, outsourcing and so much more. While all of that is important to the six-figure blueprint, it's easy to sometimes get bogged down in the details and lose sight of the big picture.

So keep this in mind: You are not here to serve the whole Etsy marketplace, change the entire world as we know it, or even to make a

$100,000. You are here to serve your ideal customer base with amazing creations that only YOU can offer them. Keep your focus on that and the six-figure income will follow.

STEP TWO: LAUNCH

Now that you've built the foundation, it's time to launch! This is the fun part where you'll set up your shop, establish your brand, create listings that sell, and start making income with your business. If you're brand new to Etsy, this is where the dream truly starts.

If you already have an Etsy shop, you'll find tons of useful information in this section that will help your shop appear more professional, expand brand awareness, improve your listings, increase profit margins, and streamline your shipping process, so you can sell more with ease. You'll learn how just a few simple tweaks to your listings alone can drastically increase your Etsy sales.

No matter where you're starting from, the launch phase is where the magic happens.

CHAPTER 3

Setting Up for Success

In this chapter, we'll cover the basics of how to set up your shop, including shop name, logo, banner, title, tagline, and more. We'll discuss shop policies, announcements, updates, and everything else you need to make your shop appear professional and appealing to your ideal customer.

How to Set Up Your Shop

Setting up your Etsy shop couldn't be easier thanks to Etsy's user-friendly website and app. Even if you've never used Etsy or any other type of e-commerce platform before, setup is a breeze.

Before we get started, just be aware that in order to open your shop, you'll need to add at least one listing to it. While you'll learn the setup process here, we recommend that you read through chapter 3 and have your first listing ready to go BEFORE you actually open your shop to make setup easier for you.

To open your shop, go to Etsy.com/sell. If you already have an Etsy account, you can create your shop by logging in. If you don't have an account, you'll be prompted to enter your email address, name, and password.

From there, you'll choose your shop language, country, and currency. Next, you'll enter your shop name and add your first listing (we'll discuss both of these soon!).

Finally, you'll set up how you'll get paid (woo-hoo!), billing, and your shop security. Once all that's done, your shop is ready to go!

Shop Name

First things first, your shop needs a name. Your name should be between 4–20 characters with no special characters, spaces, or accented letters.

Your shop name should be concise, searchable, and aligned with your brand. Resist the urge to get too creative here. The main goal of your shop name is to make it easy for customers to find you.

If you have a long name with lots of unusual words or weird spellings, it will not only be difficult for customers to find you on Etsy and Google, but it'll also be harder to generate word of mouth for your shop, when no one can remember how to spell or pronounce it. Do yourself a favor and keep it simple. Ideally, your shop name should be a reflection of your brand, the products you sell, or your ideal customer.

You'll notice that when you search on Etsy, you can click on the option to "find shop names containing [the search term]" (i.e., "find shop names containing natural soap") at the bottom of the Etsy search suggestions. If you click on this option, Etsy will bring up all the shop names containing your search term sorted by relevancy.

This means that if you can work the main product you sell into your shop name, you already have an advantage, as far as search results go. The customers who are searching for this product can be led straight to your shop from the search suggestions.

This is also another benefit of niching down, as we talked about in Step

One. When you sell just one type of product to one segment of the Etsy customer base, it's much easier for the right people to find you.

For instance, if your main product is natural soap and your general target demographic is women, then "NaturalSoapforWomen" is a good shop name for you. It's short (under 20 characters), to the point, and easy to remember. The name makes it clear what products you sell and who they're for. Women who are looking for natural soap products will flock right to you.

Of course, you don't always have to be so on the nose with your shop name. Instead of "BlanketsForBabies" (main product + who it's for), you could personalize your shop a bit more with a name like "BlanketsByBetsy" or "SleepyTimeBlankets" or something to that effect.

Remember, you only have 20 characters, so you can't get too specific here. The goal is simply for both customers and search engines alike to know what you sell and/or who you sell it to, so you can be matched with the right customer.

In the end, choose the name that feels like the best fit for you and your shop. Go with your instinct and pick what makes you happy. Just be sure the name is short, memorable, and on brand.

When you open a shop and type your chosen name into Etsy, it will tell you whether the shop name is available or not. It doesn't hurt to have multiple options on hand, just in case your top choice is taken.

One more thing to consider is whether your shop name is available as a domain name or not. A domain name is simply the URL a user types into a browser to access a specific site. For example, Etsy's domain name is etsy.com.

It can be helpful to know if your shop name is available as a domain ahead of time, just in case you want a website (like Pattern by Etsy, which we'll cover later) down the line for your business. You'll want your domain name to match your shop name, so it's not confusing for your customers.

To check if your shop name is currently available as a domain, go to namecheap.com and enter your shop name as a domain in the search bar. So for example, if your top choice shop name is BlanketsbyBetsy, you'll need to check to see if blanketsbybetsy.com is available as a domain.

One thing to keep in mind: Just because your domain name is available today doesn't mean it still will be by the time you decide to create a website. If you're really attached to a certain domain name, it may be a good idea to purchase it up front, so you know it's yours. Domain names are generally pretty cheap (less than $20 per year) and can sometimes come free with certain hosting services. We'll talk more about domains and websites in chapter 14.

There can be a lot of competition for names, so be patient and flexible until you find the one you want that's available on both Etsy and as a domain name. It may take some time, but it's worth it in the long run not to have to change your shop name later.

Shop Manager

Once you've opened your Etsy shop, you'll gain access to the Shop Manager. You'll find an icon for it on the top right of Etsy's homepage (it looks like a little craft fair booth).

This dashboard contains all the tools you'll need to manage your shop. From here, you can edit your shop, add new listings, manage orders and shipping, access marketing tools, view your stats, and so much more.

If you're new to Etsy spend some time exploring the Shop Manager and getting to know the different components. You'll be spending a lot of your time here.

If you already have an Etsy shop, you're likely already very familiar with Shop Manager, although there may be some useful tools here you've never thought to use before.

We'll be exploring these powerful tools in more depth throughout the book, so stay tuned!

Sprucing Up Your Shop

Once you're in the Shop Manager, you can edit your Etsy shop homepage to make it look professional and showcase your brand. To do this, scroll down to "Sales Channels" at the bottom left and hit the little pencil icon to the right of "Etsy."

A lot of shop owners don't make full use of the features available to spruce up their shop and make it look its best. This is a missed opportunity for sales and increased customer engagement.

While most customers will find your listings through the Etsy search results, the ones who do visit your shop want to see a professional presence that showcases what they're looking for. This increases their confidence in your shop and makes it that much more likely that they'll make a purchase from you.

The goal is for your shop homepage to clearly represent your brand and what you sell in a way that looks professional and stands out to your ideal customer.

Always keep your ideal customer in mind when you edit your shop. As you add new elements to your homepage, ask yourself, "Would this appeal to my ideal customer?" When that customer visits your shop homepage for the first time, you want it to state, without any room for doubt, "This shop is for you! this is what you've been looking for!"

If you already have an Etsy shop, use the following sections as an opportunity to tighten up on these elements, so they reflect your brand and increase buyer confidence. Look through your shop's homepage, as an objective customer seeing it for the first time and ask yourself these questions:

- Is my brand coming through consistently in all elements of my shop?
- Does my shop look professional?
- Is it clear what I sell and who it's for?
- If I was a customer in the market for _____ (whatever it is you sell), would I feel confident making a purchase from my shop?

Your answers to these questions will help you determine what can be improved upon to make your shop really shine.

Shop Icon

Let's start with the visuals: shop icon, banner, and owner photo. Etsy is a visual platform and you want your shop to stand out and look appealing to your ideal customer.

Your shop icon should be your brand logo. If you don't have a logo yet, no worries. You can have one professionally made or you can even make one yourself (no graphic design skills required!).

We'll go through each of these options now, so you can choose what works best for you.

Professional Logo

The first option is to hire a graphic designer to create a logo for your business. This costs some money up front, but ensures a professionally made logo with very little work on your part.

Start by searching for logo designers online. When you find one you like, be sure to check their portfolio, references, and prices, as well as the number of mockups and revisions you'll receive. Also, check to ensure you'll be the one to retain full ownership of the final logo once the work is complete.

We've had several custom logos designed by littlebluedeerdesign.com. We simply sent the designer a sketch with a short description of what we wanted the logo to look like and she brought it to life!

If you're on a budget, you can also find affordable logo designers on Fiverr. Just keep in mind that many of the cheaper options are made from templates, so they won't be fully original. If that's your price point though, go for it! You can always upgrade your logo later on.

DIY Logo

The second option is to create your own logo. This costs little to no money, but will take a bit of time. This is a great option for those who are new to Etsy and still deciding in which direction to take their business.

When we first started on Etsy, we made our own logo using Canva, an online graphic design tool. They have logo templates that you can customize to fit your brand.

Remember to choose colors, fonts, styles, and graphics that appeal to your ideal customer first and foremost. Keep the design elements of your logo simple and consistent. When you're done, check to make sure the logo looks beautiful to the eye, whether it's displayed on a tiny cell phone or a larger desktop screen.

PicMonkey is another online graphic design tool that's great for creating logos. It has many of the same features as Canva, including logo templates, but with different design elements. Feel free to explore the free versions of both to see which one works best for you!

Both Canva and PicMonkey offer free versions with limited features. Once you figure out which one you like best, we recommend investing in the paid version of at least one of these graphic design tools. They're typically just a few dollars a month and will come in handy for other aspects of your business later on.

Once you have your logo, it's time to upload it to your shop! Your shop icon should be 500 x 500 pixels (according to Etsy, at the time of this writing, but be sure to always check for any changes).

If you're opting for a professional logo, let your designer know that you'll need one that's 500 x 500 pixels to upload to Etsy. Most designers will provide your logo in different sizes, so you can use them across various marketing materials, such as business cards or social media.

If you're using Canva, the logo templates are already 500 x 500 pixels, so you're good to go there! If you're starting from a custom size on Canva or PicMonkey, just enter 500 for both the width and the height and set it to px.

Shop Banner

Your banner spans the top of your shop's homepage and is the most prominent graphic that customers see when they visit your shop.

It always surprises us how many shops only have an icon and no banner, as the banner is a fantastic opportunity to show off your brand and make your shop look pretty.

There are two standard-size options for banners. Big banners should be 3360 x 840 pixels and mini banners should be 1200 x 160 pixels.

Mini banners shift your listings higher up on desktop, but don't show up at all on mobile. The smaller size makes your shop icon and listings the primary focus of your homepage.

Big banners display across the entire top of your homepage on both desktop and mobile. The larger size makes the banner stand out as the primary focus of your homepage.

We recommend big banners as they have more of a "wow" factor and show up on mobile as well. They add color, branding, and pizzazz to your shop's homepage.

As with the icon, sizing guidance is based on the time of this writing, so always be sure to check the Etsy Seller Handbook at etsy.com/seller-handbook for the most up-to-date information.

In terms of graphic design, banners follow the same principles mentioned previously in the icon section. They should convey who your shop is for in a professional and appealing manner.

Your banner should match the style and colors of your icon, so they don't clash or send mixed messages about your shop. You can create banners yourself in Canva or PicMonkey or have them professionally designed.

Profile Photo

Your profile photo, also referred to as your owner photo, should be a close-up photo of you. It doesn't have to be anything fancy—just a good clear photo of your smiling face. It should be at least 400 x 400 pixels.

We know firsthand that it can be intimidating to put a photo of yourself up in your Etsy shop. Many of us are a bit self-conscious and don't want random strangers to see our actual faces. We totally get this and understand the feeling.

But here's the thing: These are not random strangers who are looking at your picture; they are potential customers. They're not here to judge you or scrutinize your photo. They only want to see that they're making a purchase from an actual human being. Your owner photo humanizes you and puts a face to your shop, so customers feel good about buying from you.

Etsy is not just another big box store run by a nameless, faceless billionaire CEO. Etsy is about unique handmade items and customers want to see the face behind those items. That's YOU.

So, don't be shy! Put your picture up and be proud of who you are and what you do. This is your shop. Own it.

Shop Title

Your shop title is located underneath your shop name when you edit your homepage. Your title is only 55 characters or less, but extremely important for both customers and search engines.

Your shop title will show up in Google search results as "Your Shop Title by Your Shop Name." So, an example would be "Hand Crochet Baby Blankets by BlanketsByBecky."

Because of this, you want to be conscious of keywords. This is the first of many times throughout the book that we will talk about search engine optimization, or SEO.

SEO is the process of increasing your site's visibility on Google, Bing, and other search engines. In short, effective SEO helps customers find your shop.

A lot of SEO is centered around choosing and properly utilizing the right keywords for your shop, products, and brand. In general, you'll want these to be specific words or phrases that your ideal customer is already searching for.

In order to find the best keywords for your shop title, go to Google and type in your main product. For example, if you sell planner stickers, then type "planner stickers" into Google.

Just like when we did our market research in Step One, Google will give you a list of suggestions based on the broad keyword you typed in. Some of the suggestions for planner stickers are "planner stickers and accessories," "planner stickers custom" and "planner stickers for adults."

Do any of these keyword phrases apply to your shop? If you primarily sell planner stickers and other planner accessories, such as bookmarks and clips, then "Planner Stickers and Accessories" could be a good keyword phrase for your shop title. Choose only the keyword phrases that make sense for your shop and let the others go.

Never use keyword phrases that don't apply to your shop, just to get customers in the door. People may visit your site, but they won't buy from you, if you don't have what they're looking for. It will only hurt your rankings, click-through rates, and credibility in the long run.

So, if you sell planner stickers but not accessories, find a different keyword phrase for your tagline. Or, better yet, add some planner accessories to your shop, since those are clearly items customers in your niche are already searching for.

If you have extra characters left after choosing your main keyword phrase, feel free to add a little extra pizzazz with adjectives or other descriptive words that your ideal customer might be searching for. In terms of "Planner Stickers and Accessories," some options might include personalized, cute, fun, colorful, practical, organizational, or custom.

Choose one to two of these descriptors that go well with your keyword phrase and add them to your shop title. Just be sure that it (a) stays under 55 characters and (b) looks good when written out and sounds pleasant to the ear. You don't want your shop title to be a mouthful (or an eyeful). It should be pithy, straightforward, and to the point.

About Section

This is the section where you get to tell your story as shop owner. It's an exciting step but can also be a bit intimidating. What are you supposed to write? We're here to help!

It starts with your story headline. This one line should sum up what you do in a straightforward but catchy way that your customers can remember your shop by. It can be as simple as "Fun Printables that Your Kids Will Love" or something more poetic like "Handcrafted Skin Care Made Straight from Nature." Whatever you choose, make it YOU.

Next, you'll write your shop story. At a minimum, your story should convey how you got started, what you do, and who your products are for. If you're feeling creative, you can also add fun facts and other relevant or interesting information about yourself, but this isn't required.

Keep in mind that although this story is technically about you, it's only about you as it relates to your ideal customer. Your story should convey who you are and why your shop is the perfect destination for the customer reading it.

Here's an example:

> Hi! My name is Jennifer and I make natural skin-care products for women who want to feel beautiful from the inside out.
>
> I started my shop in 2017 when I noticed that traditional skin-care products that I purchased in drugstores, or even high-end department stores, always made my skin break out. I wanted to try my hand at making my own completely 100% natural products that actually nurtured by skin instead of compromising it.
>
> Now, I run a natural skin-care empire of over 150 different skin-care products made entirely from organic ingredients. Each of my products is designed to help you glow and empower you to live your best life.

I've learned firsthand that when your skin looks natural and beautiful, you'll feel confident and bold from the inside out. I strive to bottle this powerful feeling and deliver it to you in every product I make.

This story is simple and straightforward. It's about the shop owner, but it's also customer-centric in that it explains what the products can do for the buyer in an enticing way. This story not only humanizes the shop owner, but also makes her ideal customer excited to try out her products. It's a win-win!

The about section also includes a space to add up to five photos and even a video. We encourage you to use all five photos to really showcase who you are as a shop owner and artist. These can be behind-the-scenes production photos, photos with family, friends, or other shop members, photos of your studio or workspace, or even collages of your products. Make these photos fun and informal. Don't overthink or stress about them too much. Just choose whatever feels best to highlight who you are and what your shop is about.

A video is optional but can be a great way to showcase your shop and brand even further. If you choose to do a video, keep it short, light, and natural.

Around the Web and Shop Members

The "Around the web" section allows you to add links for your social media channels and website. You should definitely do this, so interested customers have the option of following you. We'll talk more about social media and which channels you should focus on in Step Four.

The shop members section allows you to add another picture of yourself (this can be the same as your profile photo) and a short 250-character bio. Your bio is a chance to mention personal details that don't fit into your story.

Here's an example:

> I'm a skin-care wizard who believes in letting the natural beauty of every woman shine through with my organic products. When I'm not making skin-care magic, you'll find me baking cookies with my twin girls, working in my garden, or reading a cozy mystery book.

In just two sentences, the shop owner is able to paint a vivid picture of who they are on a personal level that customers can relate to. Again, it shows that there's a real human being behind your shop.

If you have other shop members, this is the section where you would showcase them as well.

Shop Policies

This section plays an important role in a professional shop. It sets expectations for buyers before they make a purchase and sets the standard for any issues that may come up. This includes shipping, payment options, returns, exchanges, and cancellations.

Shipping and payment are typically set to default settings by Etsy, so the only parts you'll need to edit yourself are returns, exchanges, and cancellations.

You'll start by deciding whether or not you'll accept returns or exchanges in your shop. If you choose to accept them, you'll also need to set when the buyer should contact you, when the buyer should ship the item back, and which items can't be returned or exchanged (i.e., digital downloads). If you choose to accept cancellations, you'll need to set the time frame in which you're willing to accept them.

These policies are entirely up to you and the kinds of items you sell. If you sell personalized items or skin care, you likely won't want to accept returns or exchanges at all. If you sell clothing, you may want to allow exchanges, just in case something doesn't fit. The key here is to balance your rights as a shop owner with the needs of your customer base.

Our general recommendation is to allow returns for a period of seven days after delivery. The reason for this is that we want happy customers, who don't feel forced to keep an item that doesn't work for their needs. At the same time, we want to prevent frequent and unfounded returns from picky or manipulative buyers.

We've found that a seven-day return policy maintains this balance the best. This is enough time for a customer to open the box and inspect the item to ensure it meets expectations, but not enough time for them to randomly change their mind on a whim.

A return policy often results in MORE sales because it can encourage a buyer who is on the fence to take a chance on your product. If they see that returns aren't accepted, new customers will be less likely to make a purchase from you since they haven't built up trust with your shop yet.

The goal is to always make the decision to buy from you an easy one. Allowing returns helps with this, especially when you're first starting out and don't have a lot of reviews yet.

By allowing returns in your shop policies, you've also set the expectation that the buyer will pay for return shipping, which protects you from having to pay more money when an item is returned to you. If the item isn't returned in its original condition, you won't be required to issue a full refund.

On top of that, allowing returns minimizes the chance of negative reviews. If the buyer isn't happy, there's no reason to force them to hold on to the product. As long as the buyer pays for the return shipping, you won't lose any money on the item because it can be resold to another customer for the same profit.

The exceptions to this rule are custom or personalized orders, digital downloads, and items on sale. You should never allow returns on these items.

As of October 31, 2022, Etsy allows you to set different return policies for different types of listings. This gives you the flexibility to accept returns or exchanges for some items and not others.

For cancellations, we generally recommend allowing them within one hour of purchase. Sometimes, purchases are made by mistake and this sets a simple standard for resolving issues like this.

All this being said, these are general recommendations that may not make sense for your particular shop. It may be helpful to look at the policies of other shop owners, who sell similar products to yours, to determine what the expectations are in your niche. Do your research and choose what works best for your type of product, shop, and customer base.

If you decide that you don't want to allow returns, exchanges, or cancellations at all, then don't. It's your prerogative as a shop owner, so honor that.

Shop Announcements

Shop announcements are an important but often underutilized section of your shop's homepage. They consist of one to two sentences that are clearly displayed above your items along with the date that your announcement was last updated.

To add or update a shop announcement, simply click the pencil icon next to "Etsy" under "Sales Channels" and you'll find it below "Items."

These announcements are a powerful form of communication between you and your customers. Without them, you're missing out on the opportunity to convey important messages to potential buyers.

We recommend that you update your shop announcement weekly. This shows both Etsy and your customer base that you are an active and engaged shop owner. It boosts your shop's ranking (more on this later), while simultaneously building trust with your customer base.

When updating your shop announcement, ask yourself, "What is the most important thing that I want my customers to know right now?"

You can use shop announcements to call attention to the following:

- Sales (e.g., Personalized sterling silver bracelets are 15% off this week only!)
- Specific items you want to move (e.g., Check out our incredible selection of handmade soaps!)
- New items in your store (e.g., Our newest bath bomb just dropped! Relax with a light peachy scent that's perfect for summer.)
- Seasonal or holiday items (e.g., Our all-natural lotions are a perfect present for Mom! Give her the gift of self-care with our personalized Mother's Day sets.)
- Your brand (e.g., Thanks for visiting our shop! We're here to help you discover your own natural glow with our unique selection of organic skin-care products!)
- An incentive for joining your newsletter or Facebook Group (more on this later)

While there is room to add more to your shop announcement, Etsy only displays the first two lines, so keep this short, sweet, and to the point.

Your shop announcement should never be left empty. It basically exists as a free marketing tool. If there aren't any holidays or special sales going on, you can simply add a welcome message that conveys your unique style and voice. Use it as a chance to share updates that make customers excited to buy from your shop.

Sell on Etsy App

Now that you're familiar with Shop Manager and some of the tools it has to offer, it's time to explore the Sell on Etsy app.

The Sell on Etsy app allows you to manage your shop straight from your phone, while also offering unique tools that aren't available on the desktop version of the site.

If you don't make use of the Sell on Etsy app, you're missing out on some powerful marketing opportunities, so make sure you add it to your phone ASAP. Simply download it from your phone's app store and log in!

One of the most notable features of the app is shop updates. Anyone who has favorited your shop, your items, or made a purchase from you previously will see your updates on their app home screen, as well as on Etsy.com and via links from your shop homepage.

You can also share your shop updates on social media, but we don't recommend this, since it's best to post original content to these channels. We'll elaborate more on this in Step Four.

Shop updates are a particularly great marketing tool because they're essentially just photos that link directly to your listings. This makes the selling process that much easier, as it enables customers to buy directly from the photo.

To post a shop update, take a photo using the app and tag it with a relevant listing from your shop. We recommend using behind-the-scenes or more "casual" photos of your product for this, rather than simply reusing your listing's main photo. You want something eye-catching and different that will make customers stop and pay attention. Like with shop announcements, you'll want to feature items that are new, on sale, or relevant to holidays or seasonal trends as much as possible.

Similar to shop announcements, be sure to post shop updates regularly to show both Etsy and your customers that you are an active and professional seller.

In addition to shop updates, the Sell on Etsy app allows you to view important shop information at a glance from your dashboard. The app dashboard has two main sections. "Shop overview" displays your traffic stats, open orders, and active listings, while "News and activity" shows your recent shop favorites, incoming orders, and new reviews.

There are also separate tabs for "Stats," "Orders," "Messages," and "More." If you're new to the app, take some time to familiarize yourself with it, just as you did with the Shop Manager, so you're aware of which tools are available to you.

A particularly useful one is the snippets feature in "Messages." This handy tool allows you to respond to messages quickly, even on the go, by saving your most frequent responses for use in future conversations.

Overall, the app gives you the ease and convenience of managing your shop efficiently from anywhere. Definitely make use of this!

CHAPTER 4

Listings That SELL

Listings are the basis of any six-figure Etsy shop. Without marketable listings, you can't make sales. And without sales, you can't grow your income. It all comes down to creating killer listings that stand out above the rest and entice customers to buy without hesitation.

Your listings will be displayed in the Etsy marketplace when customers search for keywords related to your products. This is where the bulk of your sales will come from.

As we've discussed previously, building a business is never about trying to appeal to everyone but, instead, about attracting a specific group of ideal customers.

Your listings are no different. The goal is not to create listings that appeal to everyone but, rather, ones that jump out to your ideal customer.

The Etsy marketplace is a busy space with hundreds, and often thousands, of results showing up for any given search term. The job of a six-figure Etsy shop owner is to create listings that stand out over all this noise and shout, "HEY! I'm exactly what you've been looking for!"

Your goal is to create listings that:

1. Capture the attention of your ideal customer in the marketplace
2. Entice them to click on the listing to learn more
3. Persuade them to make a purchase

In this chapter, we'll go through all the essential listing elements needed to turn your ideal customer into a buyer.

To create a listing, go to Shop Manager, click on the "Listings" tab, and then click "Add a listing" on the top right-hand corner. This is where you'll add your photos, title, category, description, tags, alt text, and more (all of which we'll discuss in detail throughout this chapter!).

Mastering the Algorithm

As you grow your shop, you'll inevitably hear about Etsy's ever-elusive algorithm.

While the word *algorithm* might sound techie and a bit intimidating at first, it's actually very easy to master if you understand the algorithm's main goal (hint: it's the same as yours!).

First off, what is an algorithm? It's basically just a fancy word for the process and calculations that Etsy goes through to determine the ranking of each listing in the search results. This process is not conducted by a human being but, rather, happens automatically when a customer types a search query into the marketplace.

The Etsy algorithm determines the order of rankings by analyzing two main factors:

1. Relevance
2. Quality

Relevance is established by your use of specific keywords or phrases that match what the customer is searching for, while quality refers to your shop's score.

Every Etsy shop receives an internal score based on shop completeness, reviews, on-time shipments, and the overall quality of your listings. While you won't know what your score is, following the guidelines in chapter 3 for establishing a professional and active presence in your shop will drastically improve your shop score. This is why it's important to start with the basics outlined there, in order to ensure your listings perform at their maximum potential.

Even if your keywords are spot on for the search query, if your shop lacks key sections or you never post shop announcements or updates, your listing is unlikely to rank right at the top.

When conducting searches on Etsy (or any platform for that matter), most customers won't look past the first page or so of results, so the higher you rank, the more sales you'll make.

By following the guidance in chapter 3, you're already working to increase your quality score, so the next step is to show relevance. This is where keywords come in.

Understanding the Algorithm

Before we discuss keywords, there's one crucial understanding needed to truly master the Etsy algorithm. You have to understand *WHY* the algorithm functions the way it does. Essentially, what is the algorithm trying to achieve?

The good news is the primary goal of Etsy's algorithm is largely the same as your goal as a shop owner. Etsy wants to create a high-quality platform filled with happy customers, who shop there as much as possible. In order to do this, the algorithm is designed to provide customers with the best and most relevant products to choose from. Happy customers equal more money for Etsy AND more money for you, which is a win-win.

As a shop owner, it's tempting to get caught up in making choices solely to please the Etsy algorithm. You can easily become trapped by constantly wondering what you can do to make the algorithm happy, so it ranks your listing higher. This can sometimes become an obsessive process, where you end up lost in the weeds (we've been there!).

Our advice is, don't overthink this. If your goal is to create high-quality listings with relevant keywords that ultimately lead to happy customers, your listings will automatically align with the algorithm's goal and rank above the others. Instead of wondering how to please the algorithm, focus instead on what your ideal customer is looking for.

Always ask yourself two questions when creating a listing:

1. Who is this item for?
2. How can I ensure this item shows up in front of the right customer?

The answers to these questions should be reflected in your listing title, tags, attributes, and description, so your ideal customers can easily find your product and make a purchase! We'll go through each of these in detail over the next few sections.

Another piece of advice: Never try to "hack" the system by keyword stuffing (overusing keywords to manipulate rankings), using irrelevant keywords, or engaging in other shady tactics in an attempt to gain higher placement. Customers notice these things, which will result in fewer clicks, fewer sales and, ultimately, lower rankings.

Instead, focus on what your ideal customer is looking for and how to deliver a high-quality experience for them. If you do this, your goals will be aligned with that of Etsy's algorithm and your shop will climb its way to success, one listing at a time.

If you prioritize providing an excellent customer experience first and foremost, your listings will naturally be displayed higher for the right customers, resulting in the most sales.

Keywords are King

Now that you understand how the algorithm works and how its goals align with your own, let's explore the power of the RIGHT keywords.

We emphasize the word "right" here because there is no success in picking random, irrelevant, or unpopular keywords. Your goal here is to choose the strongest keywords for your product and feature them at the beginning of the listing title.

Strong keywords are relevant, accurate, and descriptive, while also having a significant search volume. Search volume simply refers to how frequently customers type in that keyword while searching in the Etsy marketplace.

For example, let's say you make what you refer to as a "cuddly toy," but most customers would search for your item as "stuffed animal" or "plushie." In that case, you'd want to prominently feature those search terms in your listing over "cuddly toy" because they have a higher search volume on Etsy.

There are three basic ways to determine search volume:

The first way is to perform keyword research within Etsy itself. You can search for your keywords in the Etsy marketplace and see which suggestions come up at the top. You can also look at the listings of high-ranking products that are similar to yours and see which keywords are used in the titles (just make sure you don't copy their title word for word—use it for inspiration only). While these methods are certainly helpful and better than choosing your keywords undirected, they are less exact than the option we'll discuss next.

The second way is to invest in a keyword tool, such as Marmalead or eRank, that shows you detailed search volume analytics for keywords on Etsy. With these SEO tools, you can research and validate your keywords with real data and statistics. While these tools are an investment, you can use them to really improve your listings and skyrocket your sales. eRank also offers a free plan with limited capabilities, so it's a great one to start with if you have budget constraints.

The third way is to research keywords on Google AdWords or Google Trends. Both of these tools allow you to analyze the popularity and competitiveness of keywords for free. With Google AdWords, you'll have to put in credit card information to use their tools, but you won't be charged unless you actually run an ad.

Regardless of which of the above options you use, the goal is to choose keywords that have a large volume of people searching for them but low competition in the search results.

This can be difficult to achieve since popular search terms often have high competition, so the aim here is simply to choose keywords that show demand that exceeds competition.

Here are some additional tips for choosing strong keywords:

- Don't choose keywords that are too general (i.e., planner). Instead choose longer keyword *phrases*, also known as long-tail keywords, that are specific to your niche (i.e., planner for working moms). These are the keywords that shoppers are more likely to use when they're ready to buy.

- Consider all the different ways a customer may search Etsy (or Google) for a product like yours. Ask yourself, "Who is this product for?" and "Why do they want it?" Let's say you're looking to sell a growth chart for kids that's shaped like an elephant. Who would be looking to purchase an item like this? Maybe a parent who's setting up their child's nursery or a friend who's attending a baby shower. So, a few good keyword phrases for your title could be "elephant baby shower gift" or "elephant nursery decor," in addition to the obvious one of "elephant growth chart."

- Go where the research leads you. You might already have a keyword in mind that you think is perfect for your listing title, but if the data shows that it isn't a strong keyword, let it go and focus on what the research is telling you.

Once you have a list of keywords, organize them in such a way that your strongest and most relevant keyword is at the beginning of your listing title. Then, organize the rest of your keywords to fill the 140-character limit.

Here's an example:

"Elephant Growth Chart for Kids | Safari Zoo Baby Shower Gift Present Nursery Bedroom Wall Decor Height Ruler New Parents Wooden Painted"

If you can't fit all of your keywords into the title, no worries. You'll also want to include keyword phrases in your tags, description, and alt text. We'll explore each of these in detail a bit later on.

Photos Worth a Thousand Words

In addition to strong keywords, another important component of profitable listings is eye-catching photos.

Etsy is a very visual platform and, as the saying goes, a picture is worth a thousand words. As such, you should prioritize filling all ten listing photos with correctly sized, high-quality, and relevant images.

While Etsy's algorithm doesn't directly take images into account, the more that customers click and engage with your photos, the higher your listing will rank. Remember, focus on customer experience FIRST and the algorithm will reward you.

If you upload a bunch of blurry photos to your listing, even if you manage to get it on the first page of search results, you won't actually make any sales. Visually appealing photos result in more clicks, more sales and, ultimately, a more successful shop.

As we mentioned above, listing photos should be correctly sized, high quality, and relevant. The rest of this section will go through how to ensure success in each of these factors along with some expert tips for making your photos really stand out.

Correctly Sized

- According to Etsy, photos should be at least 2000 pixels on the shortest side.

- We recommend that photos be 2700 pixels wide and 2025 pixels tall, in order to maintain the 4:3 ratio of the thumbnails that currently show up in the Etsy marketplace. This ensures that your entire photo will be shown and none of it will be cut off.

- If needed, you can change the size of your photo by using Adobe Express. They have an online tool that lets you resize photos for free. Just note that enlarging photos after they've been taken can result in a loss of quality.

- Take horizontal photos in order to ensure the correct 4:3 ratio. Etsy images for product listings are slightly wider than they are tall.

- Etsy sometimes changes its sizing guidelines for listing photos, so be sure to always check their site for the most updated information. You can find their current requirements and best practices in the Etsy Help Center.

High Quality

- Natural light is ideal for taking product photos. You'll want to use the light from the sun whenever possible (morning is usually best).

- When natural lighting isn't possible, a continuous lighting kit is the next best thing. You can find some good ones for less than $100 on Amazon. You can also try a basic lightbox, if you sell smaller items.

- If you're interested in a DSLR camera, we use a Canon EOS Rebel T4i for most of our photographs. We've had this camera since 2013 and it still serves us extremely well. It's very durable and takes beautiful photos. We use the Canon EF 50 mm f/1.4 Macro USM Fixed Lens and the Canon EF-S 18-135 mm f/3.5-5.6 IS STM Lens for our product photos, since they're great for close-up photography. If you're looking for a good, sturdy tripod, we love the Manfrotto tripod kit.

- If the bullet point above sounded like total gibberish to you, don't worry! You don't have to be a master photographer to take beautiful photos for Etsy. You can take amazing photos on your phone, as long as you have the right lighting and backdrop.

- Use a simple background that really lets your product shine. You can find cheap backdrops on Amazon.

- Never use blurry, unclear, or obstructed photos in your listing. If your finger is in the way of the product, don't use that photo. It's well worth the time to retake the picture rather than appear unprofessional.

- Use photo editing software like Adobe Photoshop or Lightroom to spruce up your photos. You can find many tutorials online that show simple ways to get started with these programs. You don't have to be a graphic designer to get great results with these. You'd be surprised at how much difference a few simple tweaks to the exposure, brightness, sharpness, or white balance can make to your photos.

- If you take photos on your phone and don't want to invest in Adobe software, most smartphones have basic photo editing tools built right in. Just hit the edit button to tweak a specific photo. You can also download free or cheap photo editing apps on your phone.

- If you're serious about maximizing your income on Etsy, you may want to invest in a photography class, so you can grow your skills. When we first started out, we took a one-day DSLR class at our local photography studio. It was one eight-hour workshop that cost about $150. Just that one day alone made a huge difference to the quality of our photos. Many photography schools even offer classes specific to product photography, which is exactly what you'll need for Etsy. There are also tons of online photography classes (you can find cheap ones on Udemy).

- If you have the budget for it, you can hire a professional photographer to take your listing photos. This could be a great option as you scale and your shop becomes busier and more profitable.

- Don't forget to practice! The more you take photos and work with editing software, the better you'll get. It can be a bit frustrating at first, but with a bit of time and patience, you'll see your photos drastically improve (and your sales will improve with them!).

Relevant

- While you want your photos to be eye-catching and beautiful, you also want them to be an accurate depiction of your product.

- Never edit photos to the point where they no longer look like the actual product you're selling. If you boost the color on a pale yellow blanket to the point where it looks bright yellow in the photo, your customers will be unsatisfied when they receive it because it doesn't match the picture. This results in lost sales, returns, and negative reviews, so watch out for this when editing your photos.

- Always keep photo edits simple. The goal is for the photo to stand out more, not to change or hide the product. A few simple touch-ups are all you need.

- Be honest and transparent in your photos. Don't post photos that deliberately make your product look larger or different than it is. Your photos should be an accurate depiction of the exact product the customer will receive.

- Take clear and straightforward photos that show your product as it is. Resist the urge to get too creative or "artsy" with your photos. Your listing photos aren't a creative outlet but rather marketing materials used to sell the product.

- Show detail, scale, function, and flaws in your product photos. Never try to hide flaws in the product, especially if you're selling vintage or preowned items.

- Your photos should show off your product from all relevant angles, including front, back, sides, top, bottom, inside, etc.

- Show photos that are relevant to what the customer needs to understand about your product. Does the sweater you're selling have four pockets? Make sure you can see all four of them clearly in the photos.

- Be aware that some customers make purchases based on photos alone without reading the item's description. Whenever possible, aim to communicate a product's most important details twice in your listing: once in your description and once in your photos. As an example, you should not only list the product dimensions in your description but also show scale in your photos.

- Ask yourself: "If I was thinking of buying this item, which details would I most like to see and be aware of?" Then, take photos that showcase these specifics.

- Long story short: The more accurate and detailed your photos are, the more likely you are to make sales that result in happy buyers, five-star reviews, and repeat business.

Additional Tips for Listing Photos

- Etsy allows you to upload ten photos per product listing: one main photo and nine others. Use all ten photos and make sure your main photo really stands out. This is the one customers will click on in the marketplace to get to your listing.

- Use variation photos where applicable to show different colors, styles, etc., for the same product (e.g., if you're selling the same bracelet in gold and in silver, make sure you have photos of both in your listing).

- Choose a consistent look or theme for your photos that represents your brand. All the listing photos in your shop should have a cohesive look to them. The goal is for a repeat customer to be able to distinguish your photos from others in the marketplace without even seeing your shop name. You can achieve this by using the same background, style, or props for each main listing photo.

- Think about what would appeal most to your ideal customer when choosing your photo aesthetic. You want the style of your photos to make sense within your niche, while also making it your own. Check out the listing photos for similar best-selling products in your niche as inspiration.

- Remember, you don't need to be a professional photographer or graphic designer to create listing photos that sell. Whether you're using a DSLR camera and Lightroom or simply an iPhone and its editing tools, you CAN take beautiful photos that stand out in the marketplace. You just need to keep practicing and improving each day. You'll get there!

It's in the Details

Now that you have a properly keyworded title and eye-catching listing photos, it's time to explore the remaining listing details.

Category

You'll want to select the category that best matches your product. Try to be as specific as possible within the categories that Etsy has available.

Start by typing your main keyword into the "Category" box under "Listing Details" to see Etsy's suggestions. You'll want to niche down as much as possible. For example, if you type in "blanket," you'll see Blankets & Throws, Throws, Baby Blankets, Quilts, and Pet Blankets. If your product is a baby blanket, it's better to pick the "Baby Blanket" category, as it's more specific to your product than "Blankets & Throws."

To confirm you've picked the best category for your listing, you can browse a complete list at etsy.com/help/categories/seller.

Once you've chosen your category, a list of relevant attributes will appear. For the "Baby Blanket" category, you'll see things like material, primary color, bed size, and more. Fill in as many of these as you can. This will help the right customers find your product.

You can also include variations, if applicable, to add different colors, sizes, or styles for the same product. You'll find the "Variations" section lower down the page above "Shipping."

Description

The primary function of your description is to persuade the right customers to purchase your product. To do this, you'll want to describe your product in an accurate but enticing way.

Be sure to list out all relevant details, how the product can benefit the buyer, and anything else that your ideal customers would want to know.

Previously, Etsy's algorithm did not take keywords in the description into account for rankings. However, as of May 17, 2022, Etsy updated its algorithm to include keywords in descriptions. Due to this change, you'll want to include three to five targeted keywords in your description.

Remember to always write for your ideal customer first and foremost. Avoid keyword stuffing and always write clear and easy-to-understand sentences.

Your goal is not to please Etsy's algorithm with your description but, rather, to make the sale. Keep that in mind as you write your description, while still including a sensible amount of keywords throughout. If your keywords are relevant to the product you're selling, they should fit into your description naturally without having to force them in.

As always, check the Etsy site regularly to stay up to date on any algorithm changes.

Tags

Next, you'll have the option to add up to 13 tags to your listing. Tags are unique in that their sole purpose is to communicate to the Etsy algorithm what your item is and who it's for. Unlike descriptions or titles, shoppers don't actually see your tags.

That being said, you still want to keep what your ideal customer is searching for at the forefront of your mind when choosing your tags.

That way, Esty's algorithm can use your tags to put your listing in front of the right buyers.

In many ways, tags work similarly to your title and description. You want to incorporate relevant and specific keywords that are highly searched with comparatively low competition.

Here's how to use tags effectively:

- DO use specific keyword phrases (also known as long-tail keywords) like those discussed earlier in this chapter for your tags. You're much more likely to rank for a specific tag like "merino wool blanket" than you are for something more generic like "blanket."

- DO use multi-word phrases. Etsy allows 20 characters per tag, so don't use just one word for each. Again, "merino wool blanket" is more specific than adding "merino wool" and "blanket" as separate tags (plus now you have an extra tag to work with!).

- DO research keywords for your tags on Etsy, Google, Marmalead, or eRank using the tips listed earlier in this chapter.

- DO use all 13 tags to maximize the chance of your item ranking for more keywords.

- DO repeat the strongest keywords from your title and description in your tags to increase the likelihood that your item will rank for your top ones.

- DO use variations and synonyms of previously used keywords in your tags. For example, a synonym for necklace could be chain, choker, locket, or pendant (depending on what kind of necklace it is). Think about all the different ways customers may search for an item like yours.

- DON'T repeat words from other tags. For example, don't choose "merino wool blanket" for one tag and "merino wool afghan" for another. Mix it up, so you can take advantage of as many keywords as possible. It would be more effective to highlight material in one tag and color in another (i.e., "merino wool blanket" and "baby blue afghan").

- DON'T repeat categories or attributes. These already act as tags, so using them again is redundant.

- DON'T worry about plurals or misspellings. Etsy automatically matches those for you (i.e., if your tag is "mom planner" and the customer types in "mom planners," your listing will still come up), so there's no need to waste tags on these.

Alt Text

Alt text is a newer feature to Etsy, but has been a ranking factor on Google and other search engines for years.

Alt text is a short written description of a photo or image that makes the content accessible to blind or low vision individuals. Essentially, it helps those who are visually impaired understand what you're selling.

An example of alt text is "A tall, clear crystal vase on a wooden table. The vase is round with etchings of roses and vines across the bottom two inches from the base."

In terms of SEO, alt text is a significant ranking factor for external search engines like Google or Bing. Since search engine bots can't see photos, alt text helps them determine the content of your images. This can significantly boost your rankings, especially compared to those who don't bother to use alt text at all.

Due to this, it can be helpful to incorporate some keywords into your alt text, but only when it makes sense. Remember, the main purpose of this feature is to make your listing more accessible for the visually impaired. Your alt text should be descriptive rather than sales focused.

Write in a way that is natural and helpful without keyword stuffing. Keep your alt text short and to the point. Focus only on describing what is in the photo. Don't include the words "image of" or "photo of" in your alt text.

To add alt text to your listing photos, click the pencil icon on the lower left corner of an uploaded photo.

Make Your Listings Stand Out

Once you have your listings up, how do you organize them for the best visibility in your shop? We've got you covered right here!

Shop Sections

You'll want to start by organizing those beautiful listings into relevant sections. You can have up to 20 custom shop sections, in addition to the default "All Items" section. Your sections will appear on the left side of your shop's homepage.

The purpose of shop sections is to help your ideal customer find the exact product they're looking for quickly and easily.

Start by thinking about all the items you sell and who they're for. Then, organize your shop into sections accordingly.

Let's say your Etsy shop sells jewelry. You could organize your sections by type (i.e., bracelets, necklaces, rings), material (i.e., sterling silver, 14-karat gold, platinum), or color (i.e., white gold, rose gold, yellow gold).

You can also create shop sections by customer type (i.e., gifts for her, gifts for him) and update them throughout the year to reflect seasons or holidays (i.e., add a "Gifts for Mom" section in the month leading up to Mother's Day).

It's also helpful for most shops to have a "New Arrivals" and "On Sale" section.

When creating sections, keep in mind that you can only add each item to ONE section of your shop, so choose wisely. Even if an item falls into multiple sections, choose the section in which your ideal customer would be most likely to search for it.

To add sections to your shop, go to the Shop Manager and then to "Listings." Click "Manage" on the far right next to "Sections" and then "Add Section." A section title can be up to 24 characters long.

To add items to a section, go to the Shop Manager and then to "Listings." Click the checkbox for the listings you want in that section, then click "Editing Options" and "Change Section." Choose the section you want and then hit "Apply."

Featured Listings

You can choose four featured listings for your shop. They will display at the very top of all your items, so any customer who visits your homepage will see those first.

Your featured listings should highlight one of the following:

- Seasonal trends
- Upcoming holidays
- Items on sale
- New items
- Bestsellers
- Items that you need to move quickly

Your featured listings are the first ones customers will see, so choose them in a strategic way that maximizes sales.

You should switch up your featured listings regularly to showcase the most relevant ones. Schedule a time every month or so to change them up, so you're not still featuring Christmas items in February, when you should be showcasing Valentine's Day.

To add featured listings to your shop, go to "Listings" and click the star icon on the items you want to add.

First Page Listings

The rest of your listings will default to newest first or you can customize the order yourself. Most customers will only look through the first one to three pages of your shop, so you'll want to showcase your top items there.

You should aim to show off a wide range of your best and most popular items at different price points. The goal here is to feature as many different products as possible.

If you sell mugs, T-shirts, and posters with various designs on them, be sure to show off as many different products and designs as possible on the first few pages. In other words, if you already have a mug with design A on it, don't put a T-shirt with design A right next to it. Choose one with design B instead.

You can rearrange items in your shop by visiting the Shop Manager and clicking the pencil icon next to your shop name under "Sales Channels." From there, click "Rearrange Items" to drag and drop the listings into the order in which you'd like for them to appear. When you're done, click "Exit."

Pro Listing Tips

Here are some extra tips for ensuring your listings sell:

- In addition to a shop score, Etsy also assigns listing scores. This is based largely on conversion rate (see the last bullet point for more details on this).

- Free shipping can oftentimes give your listings a boost in search results. Customers LOVE free shipping, so Etsy's algorithm loves it too. Many customers have an expectation of free shipping due to its frequency on other shopping sites, such as Amazon, so Etsy encourages shop owners to offer it whenever possible. Just be sure to factor shipping costs into your pricing (discussed in the next chapter), if you plan to offer free shipping.

- Overall, the best way to improve your Etsy search ranking is to increase your conversion rate. Your conversion rate is simply how often visits to your listings actually convert into sales. This is why you should always focus on your customers FIRST by creating accurate and enticing listings that appeal to your ideal buyer. This will improve your rankings and sales in the long run, while also ensuring a positive experience for your customer. The average conversion rate on Etsy is 1–3%

(meaning out of 100 visits to your shop, 1–3 people will make a purchase). You can check your shop's conversion rate in the Stats section of the Shop Manager.

Congrats! You're now familiar with all the listing elements needed to stand out in the marketplace and start seeing consistent product sales.

In the next two chapters, we'll cover pricing and shipping. Both of these play a role in your listings and are also vitally important to the success of your Etsy empire.

CHAPTER 5

Pricing Like a Pro

Pricing is one of the most important aspects of running a six-figure Etsy shop. It's also one of the areas that sellers tend to struggle with the most.

Assuming the quality of your product is there and the rest of your listing is strong, choosing the right pricing is the final element that ensures products fly off the shelves in your shop.

If you price your items too high, you'll have difficulty moving your products. But if you price too low, you'll have difficulty making a profit. Or worse yet, your products could be viewed as "cheap" or "generic."

Pricing is a simple calculation that a lot of sellers tend to overcomplicate. This is why we've dedicated an entire chapter of this book to pricing strategies, so you can sell your items with ease and confidence.

In the end, pricing is simply a balance between knowing the worth of your items and understanding your customers' willingness to pay. Once you nail this concept, pricing will go from being a daunting task to an easy one.

The Simple Pricing Formula

In this section, we'll outline our easy six-step pricing formula. You'll use this formula to calculate the ideal per-item pricing for each type of product in your shop.

And don't worry. You don't need to be a math whiz to nail these steps. We've also included additional free tools like fee and pricing calculators along the way to make this process as stress-free as possible. Let's dive in!

1. Consider your costs

First things first, you'll need to calculate the cost of creating and shipping the item.

You'll want to factor in the materials used to create the item (i.e., yarn, knitting needles, and patterns) plus the materials needed to ship the item (i.e., tissue paper, boxes, and tape).

You should also factor in shipping costs, if you plan to offer free shipping for the item. If not, shipping will be paid separately by the buyer and doesn't need to be taken into account here.

You should calculate your costs PER item, so if you buy materials in bulk, divide the total cost by the estimated number of items you can make and ship with those materials.

2. Factor in other expenses for your shop

Next, factor in ongoing expenses for your shop that aren't directly related to the creation or shipping of your item. This could be the monthly cost of Etsy Plus, renting studio space, email or graphic design subscriptions, and more. If any of these costs are yearly, you can divide them by twelve to get the monthly cost.

Divide the monthly cost of these expenses by the average number of items you sell in a month (you can find this by checking "Stats" in Shop Manager). The resulting number will be the average cost of these expenses per item. Add this to the per-item cost you calculated in the previous step.

If you're new to Etsy, you likely won't have many ongoing expenses yet, so you can either skip this step or make a conservative estimate based on your planned inventory for the month.

3. Pay for time and labor

Next, you'll want to pay yourself (and any other shop members or partners) for the time and labor put into creating the item. To do this, estimate how much time it takes to create one item and how difficult or skilled the labor is.

If you're unsure what to pay yourself, it can be helpful to Google what others make for the same type of craft (e.g., "How much does a knitter make per hour?"). A good place to start is in the $10 to $15 per hour range.

As an example, if an item takes 30 minutes for one person to make at a rate of $10 per hour, then the labor cost for that one item is $5.

4. Take into account Etsy's fees

Next, you'll want to factor in Etsy's fees. Etsy charges $0.20 per listing every four months that the listing is active. Once you make a sale, you will be charged 6.5% of the listed price plus the amount paid for shipping and gift wrapping (if applicable). There's also a payment processing fee of 3% + $0.25.

If this sounds complicated, don't worry! There are several free online calculators that are specifically designed to calculate these fees for you. Here are two of our favorites:

omniprofitcalculator.com/etsy-fee-calculator/
alura.io/resources/etsy-fee-calculator

If you're running Etsy or Offsite Ads for that item, you'll want to factor this into fees, as well. We'll talk more about ads in Step Four.

5. Add your markup

Markup is simply the amount added to your item's price that reflects profit after steps 1–4 of this formula are accounted for. It's typically represented as a percentage of your item's total cost.

You'll find a ton of conflicting information and a huge range of markup percentages out there based on who you ask. We've seen anywhere from 15% to 60%.

In general, 30–40% is the sweet spot, but it's not uncommon for businesses to have markups of 50% or more.

We recommend that you start with a markup of 30% and see how your price compares to similar items selling on Etsy. If your item is priced significantly higher than others, you should consider lowering your markup. This will ensure that your pricing stays competitive.

Conversely, if your price is significantly lower than your competitors after a 30% markup, you can consider increasing it.

6. Do the math

Now that you have all the numbers, it's time to do the math. We recommend using this pricing calculator:

craftybase.com/etsy/pricing-calculator

Simply input your chosen price markup along with labor cost and material cost. Labor cost is the number obtained in step 3. Material cost is obtained by adding steps 1 and 2 together. Remember that all these figures should be calculated per ONE item.

The calculator does the rest for you, including taking Etsy fees into account automatically. The calculator will then give you a suggested price, as well as your profit and margin.

So, if your labor and material costs are $10 each and your price markup is 30%, the suggested price will be $26 and your profit and margin will be $3.08 or 11.85% of the listing price respectively.

Feel free to play around with your price markup until you reach a profit and margin that you're happy with. Just make sure your pricing is competitive compared to similar listings from other sellers.

By researching the prices of the best-selling items in your niche, you'll determine your customers' willingness to pay. If customers are already paying a certain price for a product like yours, chances are they would be willing to pay a similar price for your item.

You can also attempt to lower material or other costs to achieve a higher profit margin. You can often save money on materials by shopping in bulk, searching for discount codes, taking advantage of sales, or buying from a different retailer.

Once you're comfortable with your pricing, simply add it to your listing and give it a whirl. Don't overthink this or get caught up in what-ifs. You can always change your pricing later to maximize sales (we'll talk about that next).

Pro Pricing Tips

Here are some additional tips for ensuring you always price like a pro:

- When estimating costs, always be conservative. For example, if you think that your materials will cost $10–$15 per item, choose $15 when doing the math. The reason for this is that if you estimate $10 and the actual cost is $13, then you'll make less profit than anticipated. However, if you estimate $15 and your actual cost is $13, then you'll make MORE profit than anticipated. This is why it's always best to be on the safe side until you know for sure what your costs will be.

- Always crunch the numbers before you start making your inventory. Once you have an idea of the materials, hours, and labor that it will take to create the item (estimates are fine), follow the six steps above FIRST to ensure that the item will be profitable for you. The last thing you want is to spend 20 hours making two dozen hand-stitched gnome dolls only to find out that your expenses exceed your customers' willingness to pay. Always do the math and the research first.

- If you already have an Etsy shop, take a look at your current pricing to make sure all your items are as profitable as they can be. If an item isn't selling well, do the math and check your competitors to ensure that it's priced appropriately.

- If you need to change your pricing, set the new prices for at least 30–60 days before tweaking them again. This will allow enough time to see if this results in a change in sales. You can continue to tweak the pricing every 30–60 days until sales for that product are consistent. Don't be afraid to play around with your pricing until you find the sweet spot between number of sales and profit per item.

- Remember, lower pricing does NOT necessarily mean that you will sell more items. Etsy isn't a big box store like Walmart, where buyers are just trying to get the best possible deal on toothpaste and toilet paper. You're selling a unique handmade item that you put your heart, soul, time, and labor into. Always know your worth and price your items accordingly.

CHAPTER 6

Shipping Strategies

You have your listings up and your inventory is flying off the shelves. Woo-hoo!

So now, the question is, how do you get those beautiful handmade items of yours into the hands of your buyers? Shipping, of course!

Shipping can often feel overwhelming for new shop owners. In fact, it can even be overwhelming for those who have been running a shop for years, if they don't have the right system in place.

We've been there. As owners of multiple businesses, our very first holiday season was stressful, to say the least. We found ourselves working 10-hour days the week before Christmas just on shipping alone!

This was not okay with us. Yes, we were making a lot of money, but the reason we became business owners in the first place was to set our own hours and achieve financial freedom—not to become shipping slaves. This is when we learned the shipping strategies we're going to teach you in this chapter.

Once we figured out how to streamline our shipping process, we were able to send out hundreds of items a week with no hassle at all. No stress—just happy buyers, more sales, and increasing income! You can have that too.

In this chapter, we'll present the basics of shipping first and then share advanced strategies toward the end. Let's dive in!

Where to Start

Shipping starts with your listing. Before you've even sold a single item, you need to determine your shipping prices and processing time. To edit shipping options, scroll to the bottom of your listing.

For shipping prices, we recommend using calculated shipping throughout your store. It ensures accuracy, so there are no surprises later on. To select this, go to "Shipping prices" and choose "Calculate them for me." The shipping price for that item will be automatically calculated based on the buyer's location, the weight of the package, and the dimensions of the box.

For processing time, we recommend one to three days for the best balance between speed and feasibility, but do what works best for you. Start by choosing a processing time that feels manageable to you (you can always change it later). Be realistic about what you can handle. The most important thing is knowing you can meet the expectation that you've set for your buyers. It's better to set three-day processing and ship all your packages out on time than it is it set one-day processing and constantly fall short.

For shipping services, you'll typically have a choice between USPS or FedEx. USPS is best for most items, unless the item is especially large or heavy.

USPS First Class is for packages that are one pound or less, while USPS Priority Mail is for all other items. If you ship an item with Priority Mail, you can get free boxes and padded envelopes from the post office (more on this later).

If you live outside the US, there are many available options for shipping, including Canada Post, Royal Mail, Australia Post, Global Postal Shipping, and more, depending on where you're based. You can learn more about these shipping services in the Etsy Help Center.

We don't recommend adding a handling fee to your listing. This makes shipping appear more expensive and can deter buyers. If you followed the steps in the last chapter for pricing your product, all shipping materials should already be factored into the item's price.

Next, you'll choose the size of the box that you'll ship your item in. We'll discuss different box sizes and how to determine which ones are most suitable for your product in a later section.

Finally, you'll pack your item into the box with the EXACT packaging materials you plan to use (e.g., tissue paper or bubble wrap). Weigh your product in the box with the packaging material inside and then add that weight to your listing under "Item weight" (e.g., 1 lb. 6 oz.).

Under "Item size," you'll put the dimensions of the box you're shipping the item in (e.g., 6 x 6 x 6). Most standard boxes list dimensions at the bottom, but you may need to measure it, if you're unsure.

In terms of weighing your item, a digital shipping scale or a kitchen scale will work best. If push comes to shove though, you can use a regular bathroom or body weight scale. It may not be quite as accurate, but since shipping cost is usually based on ranges (i.e., 6.5 lb. rounds up to 7 lb., so it will cost the same to ship regardless), it usually won't make much of a difference. We used a bathroom scale for years before we finally invested in a shipping scale, so don't stress too much about this.

Also keep in mind that your item weight is listed on Etsy as ___ lb. and ___ oz., so if your scale reads 6.5 lb., you'll need to input that as 6 lb. and 8 oz.

Shipping Materials

In this section, we'll discuss the shipping materials that we recommend having on hand for a quick and easy packaging process.

Basics

- Scale (digital shipping scale, kitchen scale, or bathroom scale, as discussed in the previous section)
- Tape measure (for measuring items and boxes)
- Scotch tape (for wrapping items)
- Packing tape (for taping up boxes; heavy-duty works best)
- Sharpie (to write "fragile" or anything else on the outside of boxes)

These are the basic shipping materials that all shop owners need. We recommend buying these in bulk whenever possible. It will save you money in the long run.

Packaging

- Packing paper (typically made from brown or off-white recycled paper)
- Tissue paper (white or colored)
- Bubble wrap (regular or heavy-duty)
- Packing peanuts (the regular Styrofoam ones are banned in several states, so use biodegradable and environmentally friendly ones instead)

The packaging material you choose will be based on the type of item and how fragile it is.

Packing paper is thicker and typically used to pad boxes, so that items don't move around during shipping. Tissue paper, on the other hand, is soft and used to wrap the items themselves. You can use white tissue paper or choose a colored/decorated one to add a little fun to your packaging.

Bubble wrap and packing peanuts are only needed if you're shipping fragile items. The clear bubble wrap with smaller bubbles (< 0.25 inch) is regular, while the clear/orange bubble wrap with larger bubbles (> 1 inch) is heavy-duty.

Packing peanuts ensure that a fragile item stays safe during shipping with a layer of soft cushioning all around it. Be careful though—regular Styrofoam packing peanuts are banned in many states due to their environmental impact, so always be sure to get the biodegradable ones.

You should only use packing peanuts if you sell super-fragile items like crystal vases or champagne glasses. For most sellers, there's no need for them.

Boxes

Here are some common box sizes that are most useful for shipping. All dimensions are in inches.

- 6 x 6 x 6 – great for small items that are under a pound, such as jewelry or pinback buttons
- 10 x 8 x 6 – great for small to medium items, such as mugs or candles
- 13 x 13 x 4 – great for larger flat items, such as sweatshirts or small blankets
- 14 x 14 x 14 – great for larger items, such as vases or lamps
- 12 x 8.5 x 1 (standard padded envelope) – great for flat items, such as hardcover books and sturdy planners (just be sure your item won't bend in shipping—if you suspect that it will, you're better off using a box)

This list is obviously in no way exhaustive. These are just some of the box sizes that we've found most useful for our inventory over the years.

To find the best boxes for you, measure your items and choose your boxes accordingly. Be sure to leave at least one inch all the way around for packing material (two or more inches, if the item is fragile).

So, if your item measures 3 x 4 x 5 then a 6 x 6 x 6 box would work well. But, if it measures 4 x 5 x 6 then you would need a bigger box since the height doesn't leave room for packing material.

Labels

- Printer
- Printer paper
- Ink

If you plan to use Etsy shipping labels (which you definitely should), a printer is needed to print labels for taping onto your shipping boxes. If you don't have a printer, you can buy a used one on eBay for less than $50.

If absolutely needed, you can write your shipping label by hand with a Sharpie and pay for shipping at the post office, but you'll miss out on the 30% discount that Etsy labels offer.

In the end, you'll save more time and money in the long run by investing in a cheap printer.

Where to Buy

Here are our favorite places to purchase boxes and shipping supplies.

- Home Depot (for all materials)
- Amazon (for all materials)
- Uline (for all materials)
- Office Depot (for all materials)
- UPS Store (mostly for boxes)
- U-Haul (mostly for boxes)
- USPS Store (FREE boxes!)

We recommend choosing at least three stores off this list and comparing prices to see which one gives you the best deal for different items. For example, 10 x 8 x 6 boxes might be cheaper on Amazon, while packing tape is cheaper at Office Depot. Don't feel that you need to buy all your items in one place—go for the best deal instead. Even paying 10 cents less per box can result in huge savings over the course of a year. Also, keep an eye out for coupons, sales, and cash back to save even more.

If you're using USPS for shipping, be sure to take advantage of its free Priority Mail boxes and padded envelopes. Just be sure to ONLY use these boxes for Priority Mail (not First Class).

Labels

As mentioned above, we recommend purchasing your shipping labels directly through Etsy. You'll save 30% on shipping and make the process much easier for yourself overall.

You can purchase and print labels right from the "Orders & Shipping" tab of the Shop Manager. You'll receive automatic tracking and Etsy will take care of updating buyers and keeping tabs on shipments for you.

Trust us—this all makes a huge difference once you're at a point where you're receiving dozens or even hundreds of orders a week.

The Perfect Package

Now that you have your materials and label, it's time to package your item.

Follow the step-by-step process below for the perfect package every time:

1. Fold down the bottom edges of your box with the smaller edges on the inside and the larger ones on top. Tape down the sides and middle of the box with packing tape until it's securely shut. Tape about halfway down the side of the box for extra support. Feel free to do this taping process twice for added protection.
2. Add packing paper to the bottom of the box to cushion your item. If the item is very fragile, use packing peanuts instead.
3. Wrap the item in tissue paper and tape it at the flap with Scotch tape. If the item is fragile, wrap it in bubble wrap, as well.
4. Add additional packing paper on the top and sides (if needed) until the item is secure in the box. If your item is very fragile, use packing peanuts instead.
5. Tape down the box on all sides with packing tape until it's secure following the guidelines from step 1.
6. Print the shipping label and affix it to the top of the box using clear packing tape across the whole surface of the label. Make sure the label is fully visible.

Streamlining

All the tips and strategies we've discussed so far in this chapter will help you maintain an organized, effective, and quick shipping flow. Once you know what materials you'll need and how to package your items safely, practice makes this process smoother and faster over time.

But how do you really streamline the shipping process once the orders start flying in?

Here are the strategies that really upped our shipping game:

- *Use a uniform type of box whenever possible.* Using the same type or brand of box makes the taping and packaging process more efficient than using different kinds. You'll get into the flow more easily and work faster as a result.
- *Print your labels in bulk.* In Shop Manager, select all the orders you'd like to print labels for and click "Get Shipping Labels." This is much faster than printing them individually.
- *Make your boxes ahead of time.* If your boxes aren't premade, you'll need to fold and tape up the bottoms in order to use them (see previous section for details). You can do this the night before, so the next day, they're all ready to go. If you make boxes while watching TV or listening to music, it doesn't even feel like work!
- *Make sure you have all your shipping materials on hand BEFORE you start packing boxes.* Nothing slows down the process like starting to pack a box, realizing you're out of tissue paper, and having to run to Office Depot at 8 p.m. Always make sure you're well stocked on all materials needed to fulfill every order going out that week. Use the list of materials from earlier in this chapter as a reference to ensure you'll never fall short.

- *Keep track of all the shipping materials you've purchased.* You'll thank yourself come tax season. Our first year running our business, we "tracked" our shipping materials by saving all the receipts in a bin and not looking at them again until March. Don't be like us. Start an Excel sheet and log purchased shipping materials as soon as you buy them to save yourself time and headache down the line.

- *Research the most convenient shipping options and locations near you.* We do all our shipping at a store called Parcel Plus that's less than two minutes driving distance from us. They take packages for all carriers (USPS, FedEx, etc.), so we can ship all our items from one place. We just leave our packages on the counter and never have to wait in line, which saves so much valuable time. Before we did our research and found out about Parcel Plus, we went to USPS and FedEx separately, both of which were further away AND involved waiting in long lines. So, don't assume the most obvious option is the best one—do your research, so you can save time in the long run. There's also the option of scheduling a pick-up time through USPS, so you don't even have to leave your house!

- *If you're having trouble catching up, increase your processing time.* While it's true that buyers prefer items to ship quickly, never sacrifice quality for speed. As your shop grows, you may find yourself rushing to fulfill orders on time. If this is the case, don't be afraid to temporarily increase your handling time to allow yourself room to catch up.

- *If you're overwhelmed, recruit or hire help.* As your shop grows, you may find that fulfilling orders is no longer a one-person job. If this becomes the case, you can hire assistance or recruit friends and family to help out. Your kids might even be excited to lend a hand in exchange for some pocket money or a reward!

- *If you sell on multiple e-commerce platforms, like we do, consider investing in ShipStation.* ShipStation is a software that helps you organize and streamline your fulfillment process. This is extremely helpful if you have multiple businesses, but not necessary if you have just one Etsy shop.

Purchase Protection Program

This is a new program that Etsy rolled out on August 1, 2022, to protect sellers from losing income when shipping mishaps occur.

If your order is eligible for Etsy's Purchase Protection program, you will keep your earnings if a buyer doesn't receive their order or if it arrives damaged (the latter is eligible just once per calendar year). The program only applies to orders up to $250.

Be sure your items are eligible for this program by:

- Purchasing shipping labels on Etsy OR including valid tracking information
- Using estimated delivery dates
- Shipping your orders on time
- Packaging your items carefully
- Using accurate photos and listing descriptions

STEP THREE: OPTIMIZE

Now that you have the basic strategies down, it's time to optimize! In this step, we'll build your shop's reputation, so you can increase your sales and prepare for massive growth in Step Four.

This is where it starts to get exciting! You've already laid the foundation for your business and now you'll learn strategies to make your shop the absolute best it can be.

Before you really skyrocket your business in steps 4–6, you'll need to make sure your shop is in tip-top shape. If your shop is filled with lukewarm reviews and indifferent customers, the advanced growth strategies you'll learn later in the book will be minimally effective.

Conversely, if your shop is associated with rave reviews and stellar customer service, the same advanced growth strategies will effortlessly catapult your business to six figures and beyond.

So, don't skip this step! Reviews and customer service are the bread and butter of any successful business and need to be implemented FIRST before maximum growth can occur.

By focusing on this now, you'll guarantee success for yourself later in your Etsy journey.

CHAPTER 7

10,000 Happy Customers

Successful businesses are by and large the result of excellent customer service. When you decide to open an Etsy shop, customer service automatically becomes a top priority.

As a shop owner, your income comes exclusively from customers who purchase your products. You literally cannot make money on Etsy without customers.

While this might sound obvious, many sellers fail to keep this in perspective and then wonder why their shop isn't doing well. They don't bother to respond to messages or, worse yet, argue with customers over insignificant details. Then, they're shocked when the customer leaves a negative review.

Moral of the story: in order to be successful on Etsy (or in any business), you have to put your customer first.

Now, this doesn't mean that you let customers take advantage of you. There are ways to deal with difficult customers tactfully without giving in to unreasonable demands (more on this later in the chapter). All it means is that customer satisfaction should always be at the forefront of your business strategy.

In this chapter, you'll learn our five-star approach to excellent customer service that leads directly to happy buyers and a thriving shop.

The Five-Star Customer Service Approach

Customer service doesn't just mean being nice to your customers. It's about building trust and ensuring their satisfaction.

When a customer makes a purchase from you, the relationship between buyer and seller is immediately triggered. Your job is to support your customer during every step of the process from purchase to delivery. Remember, the goal here is always rave reviews and repeat buyers.

To help perfect your skills, we've come up with a five-star approach to excellent customer service. Each of the attributes below is one "star." Fulfill all five of these to ensure a flawless customer experience.

1. Accuracy

Be sure that your listing photos and description are completely accurate and truthful to the actual item your customer will receive. Never hide flaws (especially if you sell vintage items) and always show off important details in your listing.

Ask yourself, "If I was buying this item, what would be most important for me to know?" and then answer that question through both your photos and your written description.

Also be sure to package items securely (especially fragile ones) so they arrive to the customer in the exact same condition that you shipped them in.

2. Communication

Answer all messages in a timely manner, particularly during regular business hours (Monday–Friday, 9 a.m.–5 p.m. EST). Strive to answer messages within 24 hours on weekdays whenever possible.

Also be sure to set an away message if you'll be inactive in your shop for more than one business day (vacation, illness, emergency, etc.), so customers know not to expect a quick reply.

3. Transparency

Always be clear with customers about delivery dates, processing times, or any problems that arise.

You want to set their expectations in a clear and transparent way, so there aren't any unpleasant surprises down the line.

4. Personality

Since Etsy is made up of unique independent shops, customers love to get to know you!

There are small ways you can make customers smile, such as:

- Unique packaging (i.e., colored or patterned tissue paper)
- Handwritten or printed notes (i.e., thank you for your purchase!)
- Custom stickers or cards
- Personalized purchase confirmations and emails
- Free samples or gifts

These small personal touches create a memorable experience for customers leading to five-star reviews and repeat business.

5. Diplomacy

As a shop owner, difficulties with customers will inevitably arise. When this happens, just remember that you're not alone. This happens to all of us from time to time.

A customer isn't happy with their purchase. It didn't arrive on time or it didn't meet expectations in some way.

Do your best not to panic or get emotional. It can sting when a customer isn't happy (and not all customers are polite about it either), but just remember that it isn't personal. Always strive to resolve issues with buyers as professionally as possible.

When dealing with upset customers, try to be as understanding and empathetic as you can. Be responsive, validate their concerns, and work together to find a solution.

If a customer is being irrational, simply step away for a bit and come back to the problem when you're feeling calm and ready to handle it.

If you feel that a buyer is being disrespectful or unfair, you can always reach out to Etsy Support and ask them to step in.

The buyer may also file a case if there's an issue with their order that they are unable to resolve with you (the seller) within 48 hours. If this happens, don't panic! This can very often work out in your favor.

If you did everything right (accurate description, proof that the item was shipped on time, etc.) then Etsy won't hold you responsible for the issue.

Once again, the key here is knowing that customer complaints aren't personal. They're just business and part of the job.

Rinse and repeat the above five steps with every customer and you'll be well on your way to 10,000 happy buyers and beyond.

CHAPTER 8

Getting Five-Star Reviews

Reviews are SO important to your success as a shop owner. Your star rating is prominently displayed under all your listings in the Etsy marketplace, as well as on your shop homepage.

More positive reviews = more sales. This equation has been proven time and time again in every retail business out there.

Reviews are essentially social proof. They communicate to potential buyers how many people have purchased your items (number of reviews) and how satisfied they were with their purchases (star rating).

Think about it. If a product on Amazon has 3.5 stars with six reviews and there's a similar product that has 4.5 stars with 200 reviews, which one are you more likely to buy? Would you go to a restaurant that only had 2.5 stars with three reviews on Yelp?

A large quantity of positive reviews increases buyer confidence making it that much more likely that they'll make a purchase from you. If you have 1,000 positive reviews for your shop, a buyer can safely assume that they'll have a positive experience as well.

Your goal is to get as many five-star reviews as possible. This section will show you exactly how.

Just Ask

So, how do we go about getting these glowing five-star reviews? We ask for them!

This may sound simple, but many of us just don't think of it. We simply assume that if a buyer is happy with the product, they'll leave a positive review.

The reality though is that buyers are busy. They have their own lives filled with long to-do lists. Although they may have every intention of leaving a review, if we don't remind them, they may never get to it.

In the following sections, we'll share best practices for where, when, and how to ask for a review. This is our personal foolproof system for earning thousands of glowing reviews and a five-star shop rating.

The Five-Star Review System

Here's where (and when) to ask for a review:

1. Confirmation Email

Once a purchase is complete, buyers receive a confirmation email through Etsy.

You can customize this email to include a short review ask at the end. From the Shop Manager, go to "Settings" -> "Info & Appearance" -> "Message to Buyers."

Here, you can thank the buyer for placing an order, let them know it'll be on its way soon, and ask them to post a review once they've received it.

Here's an example:

> Thank you so much for placing an order! As a small business, we truly appreciate every single customer who orders from our shop.
>
> We're so excited for you to receive your unique handmade goody from [Shop Name]. We're currently preparing your order for shipment and you'll receive an update when it's on the way.
>
> If you love your purchase, we would very much appreciate a review once you've received it!
>
> If you have any issues or concerns about your order, please message us through Etsy and we'll get right back to you.
>
> Thanks again for your business!

Since the customer hasn't actually gotten your product yet, they won't leave a review based on this message alone. We're simply bringing the idea of leaving a review into the forefront of the customer's mind with this first step.

2. Insert Card or Note

Include an insert card, handwritten note, or printed message in the physical package the customer will receive thanking them for their purchase and asking for a review.

Here's an example:

> Thank you so much for your purchase! We're so happy that you've received your special, handmade gift.

If you're happy with your order, please take a moment to leave us a review on Etsy. As a small business, reviews make a huge difference and we truly appreciate each and every one of them.

If you have any issues or concerns, please message us through Etsy first and we'll do our best to make it right.

Thanks again for your business!

The card should be placed prominently on top of the item, so the buyer can see it right away. Be sure that it's in a place where it won't get lost in the packing material.

Pro Tip: You can also add a promo code to the card for 10–15% off the buyer's next order. This encourages repeat business! We'll discuss promo codes in detail later on.

3. Follow-Up Message

Send a follow-up message to the customer through Etsy 24–48 hours after they've received the item. Ask them if they're happy with their purchase and remind them to leave a review.

Here's an example:

Hey there! It's been a few days since you received your handmade gift from [Shop Name]. I'm just checking in to make sure you're 100% happy with your purchase.

If you are then please consider leaving a review for my shop! As a small business owner, reviews mean the world to me and help me bring more amazing products to you.

If you have any issues at all with your order, please contact me right away and I will do my best to make it right.

Thanks again for your purchase.

This message is particularly effective because it allows you to get ahead of any issues the buyer may have with the order BEFORE they post a review.

Just as it's important to ask for positive reviews, it's also essential to prevent negative reviews by working with the buyer privately to solve their issues first. By checking to see if they're satisfied with their purchase, you're providing a personal touch that encourages the customer to leave a review if they're happy or reach out to you if they're not. It's a win-win.

The above system works so well because it reminds the customer to leave a review in each of the three stages of the buying process: right after purchase, when the product is received, and immediately after.

One important rule to follow: Only ask for a review ONCE in each stage. Never spam or overwhelm the buyer with too many review requests. In this case, more is not better.

Pro Tips

- *Be personable.* Show off your unique personality through your review ask and aim to connect directly with your ideal customer. If buyers feel like a friend is asking for the review, they'll be more likely to leave a sincere one.

- *Be genuine.* Ask for reviews because you honestly want to hear customer feedback and not just so they can boost your shop rating. If you become desperate in this process, customers can sense that and they will be unlikely to leave a (positive) review.

- *Don't be shy!* It can feel awkward to ask at first, but with practice you'll get comfortable with this system. Most buyers are happy to leave reviews for purchases that they're satisfied with. All you need to do is ask.

- *Never be pushy or spam buyers about leaving reviews.* Send each review ask listed above one time and then let it go. Many buyers won't leave a review and that's totally fine. There are plenty of others who will. Don't chase.

Negative Reviews

An occasional negative review is expected in this business. Even if you create flawless products, ship them out on time, and follow our review system to a tee, you could still receive a rare less-than-stellar review.

Rest assured that a few negative reviews won't hurt your business one bit. As long as your number of five-star reviews far outweighs the rest, you'll be just fine.

Unlike most other platforms, Etsy only allows users to sort reviews by "Suggested" and "Most Recent." This means that most customers will never even see your negative reviews.

All customers really see is the average review rating for your shop. As long as most of your reviews are positive, you'll be able to maintain a five-star-overall rating without issue.

When you receive a negative review, you should follow the steps below:

1. *Don't take it personally.* Yes, a negative review stings, especially when you work so hard to provide the best products and service out there. Just remember that this isn't a reflection on you. The customer is reviewing a product, not you as a person.

2. *Try your best to make it right.* Reach out to the customer privately and discuss a solution. This might mean offering a partial refund, exchange, or even a full return. Once you've solved the customer's problem, reach out via message and ask if they'd be willing to edit their review. Most customers are happy to do so, but you should never insist or be pushy about it. Just ask once and then let it go.

3. *Consider responding to the review.* If you feel like you've done everything you can to make it right and the buyer hasn't changed their review, you can consider responding to it. Your response will be posted publicly and can be a positive way to show other buyers that you're an active and professional shop owner. Just make sure your response is honest, polite, and not emotionally charged in any way. The goal is to address the specific concerns mentioned in the review and explain the steps you took to remedy them. Just be aware that once you post a response, the buyer won't be able to change their review anymore, so make sure you go through option 2 first.

4. *Check for patterns.* One or two isolated negative reviews is nothing to be concerned about. However, if you're receiving a number of negative reviews, especially ones that bring up the same issue repeatedly (e.g., the clasp on this bracelet breaks after one week), then it's time to listen to the feedback and amend your product or shop accordingly. Again, this isn't a reflection of you as a person. You're simply using negative reviews as an opportunity to improve your shop. Consider them free,

constructive feedback for your business and take them into consideration without taking them to heart.

5. *Let it go.* Sometimes, you'll receive a review that is rude, hurtful, and not constructive at all. In this case, just let it go. This review says everything about the person who left it and nothing about you or your shop. Step away and let it be. You don't need that kind of negativity in your life.

6. *Report policy violations.* If you think that a particular review violates Etsy's policies, you can report it and they may remove it for you. You can find out more about Etsy's review policies on its website.

STEP FOUR: GROW

You've made it to Step Four! Here, you'll learn all of our best marketing strategies to grow your business faster than you'd ever thought possible.

This is the secret sauce of any six-figure business. It's where your Etsy shop will soar to new heights, as your income starts to climb toward the $100,000 mark and beyond.

This is so exciting! Let's get started.

CHAPTER 9

Marketing 101

Before we share our detailed marketing strategy for Etsy, we wanted to include a short chapter on basic marketing principles.

Through years of experience in the online business space, we've consistently found that those who have a firm understanding of these principles tend to have the best results, whether it's through social media, email, or paid advertising. We want you to have a good command of these principles too, so you can multiply your results without needing to multiply your efforts.

As you go through the rest of Step Four keep these principles in mind and you'll be well on your way to a booming Etsy shop.

The Purpose of Marketing

A key principle that many people don't fully grasp when it comes to marketing is its true purpose. Believe it or not, the purpose of marketing isn't simply to get customers into the door of your shop.

The purpose of marketing is to provide standalone value for consumers through content, with the long-term goal of strengthening brand awareness and increasing sales.

In other words, six-figure marketing isn't about making the quick sale. A few quick sales won't build a sustainable income. Instead, your goal is to develop your brand and build trust with your ideal customer base.

Ultimately, you want your shop to become a hot spot for consumers in your niche. Once this happens, they will buy from you automatically and you will build a strong business that generates a six-figure income year after year.

All of this is accomplished by providing valuable marketing content that shows authority in your niche and effectively demonstrates how your products will benefit your ideal customers. We'll explore this more throughout the next few chapters.

It's Not About You

One of the first rules of marketing: It's not about you. It may be your shop and your products, but a successful business focuses on the customer first.

Your customer's primary concern will always be what you can do for them. They're not going to make purchases as a favor to you but, rather, because your marketing has led them to believe that your products will benefit them in some way.

As such, all the content you create for your shop must be customer focused. Your marketing has to provide value as it applies to your ideal customer.

For example, let's say there are two different meditation bloggers, both of whom are selling a 30-day meditation program. The first blogger talks on and on about how great she is at meditation, name-drops all the so-called meditation gurus she's studied with, and posts countless selfies of herself meditating in her bedroom. The second blogger shares a detailed step-by-step guide on how to meditate, provides useful tips, answers questions, and posts free meditation videos.

Assuming the price and content of the two programs are the same, which blogger are you more likely to make a purchase from? The answer feels obvious.

The second blogger provided valuable content that was relevant to you. She demonstrated her knowledge and teaching style, so you can trust her to deliver a meditation course that's applicable to you and your goals.

As this example shows, providing customer-focused value is a very powerful form of marketing when used appropriately.

Value

As shown in the previous section, marketing isn't just about showing off your product. It's about providing value to the customer before they've even made a purchase.

While Coca-Cola can show off its latest product and make instant sales, they're a well-established brand that's already built up decades of trust with consumers.

Small businesses, especially new ones, need to work a bit harder to build trust with their customers. The quickest way to achieve this kind of loyalty is by providing value within your marketing efforts.

As an Etsy shop owner, you can provide value by showing off behind-the-scenes photos on Instagram, engaging with members of your Facebook Group, sending an exclusive coupon to your email list, and much more.

If you really want to kick it into high gear, you could even start a blog and share content that's related to the items you sell. For example, a shop owner who sells crochet patterns could start a blog teaching others to crochet. The blog could include basic crochet projects for free with links to purchase more intricate patterns from their Etsy shop.

This provides value to potential customers first, while also encouraging them to make a purchase. It's also a great way to get prospective customers to join an email list (we'll discuss email marketing in chapter 11).

While a blog is a larger time commitment and certainly NOT required for building a six-figure Etsy shop, it does have the potential for huge returns, if it's something you're interested in.

The point is that providing value can be big (like a blog) or small (like a behind-the-scenes photo). You can put as much or as little time into this as you'd like. Whether you choose to spend hours a week or just a few minutes a day on this, the most important part is to stay consistent.

Consistency

As with almost anything in life, consistency leads to success.

If you post on social media five times in one day and then don't post again for two weeks, you won't get very far. But if instead, you make an effort to show up in front of your customers regularly, they will reward you with regular sales. It's really that simple.

Remember that a little each day goes a long way. An effective marketing strategy takes very little time, as long as you're consistent with it.

CHAPTER 10

Six-Figure Social

Now that you're familiar with our marketing principles, let's dive right into social media. Social media is a free and absolutely essential way to generate buzz and sales for your shop.

Confession: We're not big fans of social media and barely use our own Facebook and Instagram profiles in our personal lives. That being said, we use social media ALL the time for our businesses because it's a necessary part of a six-figure marketing strategy.

It's practically impossible in this day and age to build a successful business without social media. So even if, like us, you're not a big fan of these platforms personally, you should still use them for your business.

Trust us—it pays off big time.

The Six-Figure Strategy

Social media is all about connection, which allows you to build brand awareness and loyalty within your customer base.

Our approach to six-figure social media is a simple three-part strategy. All three parts work together concurrently, as well as build on one another.

We'll explore each part in turn throughout the next few sections, but here are the basics:

Part A: Choose one social media platform that allows for personal connection and engagement with your ideal customers.

Part B: Choose one social media platform where the audience is already looking to make purchase decisions.

Part C: Focus 90% of your social media efforts on growing and nurturing those two platforms.

If you follow our approach exactly, you can consistently grow your customer base in just a few hours a week. Over time, these strategies will drastically increase your sales and help you reach six figures practically on autopilot.

Part A: Facebook Groups

This part of the strategy involves choosing a social media platform that promotes personal connection and engagement.

Since our overall strategy centers on only two main platforms, you'll want one of those platforms to be a place where your customers can get to know you. This is the quickest way to build loyalty and trust, leading to a customer base that buys from you over and over again.

As we mentioned in the previous chapter, we're not chasing one quick sale here. The goal is to create a space that encourages repeat buyers. You want your ideal customers to keep coming back to your shop for more.

The best way to do this is to start a Facebook Group. And no—this isn't the same as a Facebook Page. Groups are for engagement, while Pages are for business.

So, why wouldn't we focus on Facebook Pages then? After all, we're running a business here, right?

And that's precisely the problem. Similar to when we explored the Etsy algorithm, we need to look at Facebook's overall goals as a platform. They're a social network and their purpose is to promote community, engagement, and friendship on their channel.

This is why Facebook Pages, which are designed for business purposes, get terrible reach. Reach is the number of users who see a post from your Page, either from their feed or from visiting the Page itself. If you publish a post and the reach is three, this means that only three people have seen your post.

Pages get very low reach because Facebook knows that their users don't like seeing a bunch of businesses on their feeds. They want to see posts from their friends, family, and community. This is the main reason Groups get much better reach than Pages.

Another reason is that you can run ads from a Page to increase your post reach. Facebook wants business owners to pay for these ads and knows that lower reach incentivizes them to do so. You can't run ads within Groups, which results in much higher organic (aka nonpaid) reach by default.

Groups are also specifically designed with the purpose of higher engagement. Engagement is the number of people who liked, commented, or clicked on your post. With more engagement, the Facebook algorithm will show your post to more people leading to even better reach. Overall, Groups are the clear winner here.

That being said, you can, and likely should, still have a Facebook Page for your business. This helps build awareness and legitimacy. Just don't focus the majority of your efforts there, when you could be using that time to nurture your Group instead.

If you have a Facebook Page for your shop now and are only getting 24 views on a post even though you have over 1,000 followers, low reach and engagement are the culprits. This is why we're encouraging you to start a Group for better results with the same amount of effort.

As we've said, Facebook Groups are all about engagement. When people post in a Group they're typically asking questions, answering questions, or discussing a topic that they're excited about. By starting your own Group, your niche, shop, and products will become that exciting topic of conversation.

To sum up, we recommend building an engaged Facebook Group, as a core part of this strategy, because it's the best platform for fostering relationships and gets much better visibility than Pages.

Plus, despite the growth of newer channels like Instagram or TikTok, Facebook still remains the largest social media site in the world with nearly 2.5 billion monthly users. In fact, Facebook Groups alone are used by 1.8 billion people worldwide every month. Go where the people are.

How to Start Your Group

Groups are completely free and all you need is a Facebook profile to start one. Facebook has an easy step-by-step guide for starting a Group in their Help Center.

Once you start your Group, you'll find a number of Admin tools that will allow you to post, moderate, and accept new members into your

Group. Take some time to explore these thoroughly, so you know what's available to you. If you get stuck or want a more in-depth view, there are tons of free tutorials available on YouTube.

Start by choosing a Group name (something relevant to your Etsy shop/niche), uploading a banner photo, writing your About section, and setting Group rules (e.g., no spam). You should be clear about the purpose of your Group and be sure to highlight your Etsy shop throughout.

For example, you could start your About section with "Welcome to [Your Group Name]! This is a supportive community for those who are passionate about all things crochet, hosted by [Your Name] of [Your Shop Name]."

After you're all set up, invite at least ten friends to join your Group who you believe will be genuinely interested in what you have to offer. Please do NOT spam invite your entire friend list. If they're not interested in what your shop or Group has to offer, they will either leave the Group or, worse yet, simply not engage, which will kill your reach. Your goal here is to grow a group of engaged potential customers, not a random group of high school friends and distant cousins.

We'll talk more about how to grow your Group later on. For now, just invite a few people to join who you know are already interested in your product or shop, so you have Group members to start engaging with.

How to Engage Your Group

The primary purpose of your Group is engagement—not sales. If you foster a genuine connection with your Group members, it will naturally lead to consistent sales for your shop over time.

If however, you approach your Group with the sole intent of making money, you will appear "slimy" or "salesy" and members will leave your Group faster than you can say, "WAIT!"

Always remember that we're not chasing a one-time sale here. We're playing the long game to reach six figures in the shortest amount of time. It sounds paradoxical, but it works.

Your Group should be a fun and welcoming place that your ideal customer wants to spend time in. The goal is to build a community of super fans, who will buy from you over and over again. Once you've achieved this, you'll never have to worry about sales; they'll just happen automatically every time you post in your Group.

Once they get to know you, you'll be able to count on Group members not only for sales but also for positive word of mouth and even market research. You can engage with your Group by asking questions, sharing updates, and providing value. You can run polls floating new product ideas and get feedback before you even start creating anything. It's a great way to learn more about your ideal customers, so you can build your tribe and make your shop even better.

Remember, your Group isn't about you. Focus instead on providing real value to your ideal customer and the sales will follow.

How to Sell to Your Group

As you've probably figured out by now, you sell to your Group by engaging with them. This is where you'll put the marketing principle of providing value into practice.

Ideally, you'll want to post in your Group at least three times a day for maximum engagement. Not every member of your Group will see every post, so while you never want to be spammy, you don't have to worry too much about overwhelming your audience either.

You'll want to share a mix of engagement posts (just value) and engagement + promotion posts (value + sale). All your posts should be relevant to your Etsy shop but presented in a non-salesy way.

Engagement posts should encourage Group members to like, comment, or click on the post.

Here are examples of engagement posts for various niches:

> Rose Gold. Yay or Nay? [Jewelry Niche]
>
> As promised, here's a photo of my at-home pottery studio! What do you think? [Pottery Niche]
>
> I'm working on my latest T-shirt design! What would you be most excited to wear? [T-Shirt Niche] (This is a poll where you would present various design options and ask Group members to vote; this is part engagement and part market research.)
>
> My golden retriever, Max, loves to lie at my feet while I crochet. Share a photo of your fur baby in the comments below. [Crochet Niche] (A post like this helps Group members get to know you, while still staying relevant to your niche.)

Engagement + promotion posts should still engage your Group members, while also explicitly mentioning a product they can purchase. Be sure these are direct but not too salesy.

Here are examples of engagement + promotion posts for various niches:

I'm SO excited to show you my brand-new rose gold rope necklace! What do you think? [Jewelry Niche] (Add a photo of the necklace to your post and a link to your listing in the comments. Never post outside links directly in your posts; they can kill your reach by up to 50%, as the algorithm dislikes anything that takes users away from the Facebook platform.)

Hard work pays OFF! The three-story miniature dollhouse I've been working on for the last two months is finally live in my shop. Can I get a woo-hoo? [Miniatures Niche] (When creating a new product, you can post progress photos throughout the process, so customers are excited to see it form. That way, when the new product hits your shop, they'll already be revved up to buy it. This is especially true if your Group already validated your new product idea through a poll earlier on, making them feel directly involved in its formation.)

BOO! What are your favorite Halloween traditions? For me, it's making a cute crochet pumpkin to add to my collection. You can find the pattern in my shop! [Crochet Niche] (Add a photo of the finished crochet pumpkin to the post and a link to buy the pattern in the comments. Be sure to take advantage of seasonal trends or holidays in your posts!)

Did you know that March is National Crochet Month?? Celebrate with 20% off any crochet pattern in my shop by using the code MARCH at checkout. This special discount is only available to members of this Group to show my love and appreciation for all of you. Thanks for being here! [Crochet Niche] (Offer the occasional exclusive discount available only to your Facebook Group. This makes your members feel special and appreciated. We recommend offering these exclusive coupon codes about 3–4 times per year.)

How to Grow Your Group

In this section, we'll share many effective strategies for growing your Facebook Group. Before we get started, just be aware that while a larger Group can result in more sales, what matters most is the number of ENGAGED members in your Group. The number of people in your Group is just a vanity metric, if no one is buying.

The members who don't read, like, or comment on your posts will eventually stop seeing them and are highly unlikely to make a purchase from your shop. This is why spam inviting random people is not on our list of recommended ways to add new members to your Group.

You should instead aim to grow your Group in a purposeful way to include current and potential customers who have a genuine interest in your Etsy shop. The more engaged members you have, the more sales you will make. Period.

Here are the MOST effective ways to grow your Facebook Group:

- Mention your Facebook Group in order confirmation emails and insert cards/notes in your packages (in the same places you asked for a review in the previous step). Those who have already bought from you are the ones most likely to join and engage with your Group.

- Mention your Facebook Group in your Shop Announcements, About section, and anywhere else that makes sense within your Etsy shop (just don't overdo it). If someone has visited your Etsy shop but hasn't made a purchase yet, an opportunity to join your Group is a great way to nurture them into becoming a customer.

- Mention your Facebook Group to your email list. While your email list is a great marketing tool in and of itself (more on this later), your marketing efforts are amplified when the same customers engage with you on multiple platforms.

- Post about your Group on other social media channels, including your Facebook Page or Profile, Instagram, or Pinterest.

- Use special events and giveaways to incentivize new people to join. For example, you could run a giveaway for a free product from your shop only for members of your Group (i.e., if you join the Group by 7/12 at 11:59 p.m. ET, you'll be automatically entered to win a free rose gold pendant from [Your Shop Name]). Use the ideas from this list to advertise your giveaway in as many different ways as possible. Announce the winner in your Group.

- Encourage existing members to invite friends to join the Group by running a giveaway (the number of entries each member receives is based on how many of their friends join the Group during the giveaway period). Just be sure to remind Group members to only invite friends who are genuinely interested in your niche.

- Run Facebook Ads to promote your Group. We've had consistent success with running cheap Facebook Ads to grow our Group, usually to advertise a giveaway or special event like the ones mentioned above. Facebook advertising is a huge topic that is outside the scope of this book, but there are many resources and classes out there about Facebook Ads, if you're interested in learning more. Please note that you must have a Facebook Business Page that is associated with your Group in order to run an ad (you can't run paid ads from within your Group).

Once you've decided where and how you'll advertise your Group, entice potential customers to join by using language that speaks to what the Group can do for them.

Here are two examples:

> Join [Group Name] by [Shop Name] on Facebook to access exclusive behind-the-scenes photos, new product updates, and special discounts that are only available to Group members!

> Join [Group Name] by [Shop Name] on Facebook to bond with a whole tribe of amazing women, just like you, who love crochet and are always on the lookout for that exciting new project!

Best Practices for Facebook Groups

- *Never add links directly to your posts.* This drastically decreases your reach and lowers engagement. Instead, add links in the comments or, better yet, write out the URL for your shop homepage in your banner photo. You can add any products you mentioned in your Group to your featured listings on Etsy, so members can find them easily when they visit your shop.

- *Stay away from words like "sale," "free," "buy," "sign up," or anything else that sounds like self-promotion.* Again, Facebook lowers reach on posts like these because their algorithm prioritizes engagement over blatant calls to action. Remember, your main goal on Facebook is to build your brand by creating interactive posts that foster trust and connection. If you follow the guidance in this chapter, you'll be able to effectively sell to your members without using salesy language.

- *Make an effort to pop into your Group 1–2 times per day to answer comments and engage with customers.* Show up regularly, but don't obsess and check in on your Group 24-7. A good rule of thumb is to pop in once at the beginning of the workday and once at the end.

- *Be consistent.* Aim to post in your Group at least three times a day, most days of the week. You can schedule your posts in advance using the "Scheduled Posts" feature in the Admin tools. You can also use an external social media scheduler like Hootsuite or SocialBee. Once you get used to this process, you'll be able to schedule a week's worth of posts in just 10–15 minutes.

- *Make members feel special.* Your Group members are your tribe and likely to become your most loyal customers. Treat them like they're extra special VIPs (because they are) by occasionally offering exclusive discounts, product previews, and other goodies, just for them!

- *Be aware of sweepstakes and contest rules.* If you choose to run a giveaway or contest to grow your Group, make sure you research all the rules and laws pertaining to these before getting started. A big one to be aware of is "no purchase necessary," which prohibits you from requiring that users make a purchase in order to enter.

Part B: Pinterest

While Facebook Groups allow you to connect with your customers and foster a sense of community, Pinterest is the platform where users are most likely to become first-time buyers. A whopping 90% of weekly users make purchase decisions on Pinterest, while 77% have discovered a new brand or product on Pinterest.

Facebook Groups promote customer loyalty, leading to increased sales from existing buyers over time. If you grow and nurture your Group consistently, you will eventually receive a large volume of sales from members, especially when you launch a new product.

Pinterest, on the other hand, allows you to get your products out in front of new customers who are already primed to buy just by being on the platform itself.

How Pinterest Works

While Pinterest is considered "social media," it operates more like a visual search engine. The user types a search query into the box and receives a large batch of relevant Pins to look through. Pinterest also has a feed that shows users Pins related to their interests and previous searches.

If you're new to Pinterest, a Pin functions as a visual bookmark, which a user can either save to a Board for later or click through to visit the linked site (i.e., your Etsy shop), right then and there. A Board is basically just a way to organize Pins into categories (e.g., "Decorations for Baby Shower" or "My Favorite Necklaces"). By saving a Pin to a Board, the user is essentially bookmarking the link to visit at a later time, as well as sharing the Pin with their followers and across Pinterest's feed as a whole.

The goal is for your Pins to show up in front of as many of your ideal customers as possible. Popular Pins result in consistent sales, while viral Pins can lead to massive revenue spikes for your shop.

In order to achieve these targets, you'll want to perform keyword research, create eye-catching Pins, and schedule your Pins throughout the day for optimal effectiveness.

The Pinterest Strategy

We recommend creating your Pins in Canva and then scheduling them using Tailwind. Tailwind is a Pin scheduler that allows you to preschedule your Pins to post on Pinterest at regular intervals throughout the day. This ensures that your Pins are constantly being shown to the right customers.

We love Tailwind because you can simply "set it and forget." Similar to scheduling your Facebook Group posts, you can batch schedule your Pins once a week and then sit back and watch saves happen on autopilot. This is significantly easier and more effective than trying to schedule Pins manually throughout the day.

The title, description, and alt text for your Pin are what the Pinterest algorithm uses to determine who your Pin is for and where it will show up on the platform. Similar to Etsy, your goal is to use accurate and descriptive keywords that appeal to your ideal customer.

You'll perform keyword research for Pinterest the same way you do for Etsy, by looking at search suggestions and analyzing titles of similar Pins, along with all the other strategies outlined in chapter 4. As always, be sure to use a good amount of relevant keywords without stuffing.

Another option is to simply use the SAME keywords from your Etsy research to save time. Your keywords will likely be similar between both platforms, so a quick Pinterest search will validate whether or not the same keywords will work for your Pin.

Your Pins should be eye-catching and the correct size (1000 x 1500 pixels) so they pop on users' screens. Be sure to check Pinterest's current best practices for Pins, as sometimes the recommendations change.

Canva has a lot of amazing Pin templates that you can use to create a variety of Pins quickly. You'll want to create multiple Pins for each product, as opposed to sharing the same Pin over and over again. Use different product images and text, so the Pinterest algorithm sees the Pin as "fresh" and shows it to more users.

If you create new Pins regularly and Pin consistently using Tailwind, your account will soon gain major traction, rewarding you with new customers and a continual boost in sales. You can then funnel those new customers into your Facebook Group, using the growth strategies from the previous section, to nurture them for repeat business. You can even create Pins directly to your Facebook Group for a continuous influx of new members (e.g., Join our free Crocheting Community for patterns, project ideas, support, and more!).

See how this all works together? This is why we recommend one platform for engagement (Facebook Groups) and one for new customers (Pinterest). Many of the members of your Facebook Group will be customers who previously bought from you on Pinterest and are looking for more engagement with your brand.

The two platforms work together synergistically when used correctly and consistently. We definitely recommend using both for maximum growth and supercharged sales for your Etsy shop.

Best Practices for Pinterest

- *Create a Pinterest business account.* We recommend using a Pinterest business account for this strategy, as opposed to a personal one. A business account is free and has useful features, such as access to analytics, the ability to run Pinterest ads, and the addition of a Shop tab. You should check your analytics regularly to measure the effectiveness of your Pinterest strategy and make any necessary tweaks to increase your success.

- *Create relevant Boards.* To get started on Pinterest, you should create at least ten Boards that are relevant to your niche. To find the best Boards for your niche, type your main keyword into Pinterest search. At the top of the search results, you'll find colorful tiles with a related keyword on each one. For example, if you search "jewelry," you'll find words like "beaded," "bridal," "gold," and more. If you click on "beaded," your search term will change into "beaded jewelry" and you'll receive a whole new slew of tiles with words like "black," "homemade," "seed," and more. Use these search word suggestions to create relevant Boards for your account. Just make sure you have products in your shop that match the Boards you're creating (i.e., don't create a Board for "Beaded Jewelry" if you don't sell this item in your shop). You can also use these word tiles for keyword research when creating Pins.

- *Occasionally save relevant Pins that are not your own to your Boards.* While you want to mostly save your own Pins to your Boards, you should also occasionally save Pins created by other users as well. This creates more diversity in your account and can lead to more followers. Just make sure the Pins you're choosing are relevant to your niche, ideal customer, and brand.

- *Utilize Group Boards and Tailwind Communities to expand your reach.* Group Boards are collaborative Boards that multiple users can save their Pins to. The Board is owned by one Pinterest user, who has given others permission to add Pins to that Board. Group Boards widen your reach on Pinterest and allow you to share your products with an untapped market that's likely larger than your own. You can find Group Boards to join by typing keywords that are relevant to your niche into the search bar and filtering it to just "Boards" (you can find the filter on the upper left-hand corner by the word tiles). Find relevant Boards with multiple collaborators and reach out to the owners politely asking if they'll invite you to join that specific Group Board. You can also find a directory of Group Boards here: pingroupie.com/boards. Tailwind Communities is another collaborative tool that allows community members to share each other's content in an effort to get more eyes on their Pins. We recommend using both Group Boards and Tailwind Communities to grow your account and bring in new customers.

Part C: The 90% Rule

This part is all about focus and consistency. It's what we call the 90% rule of social media marketing.

The 90% rule states that you should concentrate 90% of your efforts on the TWO social media platforms that result in the MOST amount of sales.

When it comes to social media, we often feel the need to be everywhere at once. We want to be on Pinterest, Facebook, Instagram, TikTok, and Twitter all at the same time. Plus, with new platforms constantly popping up, it's easy to get shiny object syndrome and jump ship to the hot new thing.

Please resist the urge to do this. Not only will you feel overwhelmed, but you'll also spread yourself too thin and your efforts will be ineffective. If you jump around between six different platforms, you'll never gain solid traction on any of them and end up back at square one a year later.

It's much better to concentrate most, if not all, of your efforts on just two platforms. Show up on those two platforms consistently and focus on growing them. We promise, you will be rewarded with increased sales for your shop faster and easier than if you spread your efforts all over the place.

One sale from Instagram and one sale from Twitter won't build you a six-figure shop. But a constant influx of repeat business from a well-nurtured and growing Facebook Group fueled by new customers found on Pinterest will get you there.

You need to have a cohesive strategy with social media. You can't just randomly post here and there on six different platforms and expect to grow. It's much better to post three times a day on one platform than once a day on many platforms. More is NOT better when it comes to marketing. Focus and consistency are the keys. Always.

If you do choose to have other forms of social media, you should primarily use the other platforms to drive more customers to your two main platforms. For example, using your Facebook Business Page to drive traffic to your Facebook Group.

Other than that, focus on the two main platforms that bring you the most sales and don't look back. In one year, you'll gain much more growth and income for your shop with two well-maintained platforms than with six mediocre ones.

Ask yourself where you want your shop to be in one year and focus on getting there without distraction. That's how you win at social media marketing.

Other Platforms

While we've experienced the highest growth in sales from Facebook Groups and Pinterest, each shop owner is different. You may already have another platform in mind for your business and that's totally fine.

The truth is that the platform you choose is less important than following the two rules below:

1. Stay consistent
2. Choose just two platforms and focus on those (the 90% rule)

If you're consistent and focused on two main platforms, resisting the urge to be everywhere at once, you are much more likely to succeed, no matter which platforms you choose.

A common social media platform for Etsy is Instagram. This platform is extremely visual, which is great for showing off products. Photos and videos typically get a lot of likes and comments, plus it's fairly easy to grow your account simply by posting.

The issue with Instagram is that users rarely leave the platform. They scroll through their feed and like a bunch of stuff, but they aren't very likely to click through to your actual listing. Instagram doesn't allow links in its posts, so users have to either visit your profile to get the link or physically type it into a browser themselves. Sadly, most people just aren't going to go to that amount of effort to visit your shop.

While it's easy to post on Instagram, add the right hashtags, and get tons of attention on your posts, likes and comments don't mean much if they aren't resulting in sales. Looks can be deceiving and it's not uncommon for a post with 100+ likes to result in zero sales. Keep an eye on your Etsy analytics (more on this in chapter 13) to see how many of your shop visits are actually coming from your Instagram posts. Then, decide if the time you're spending on the platform is worth your while.

Pinterest, on the other hand, is also very visual AND the Pins are specifically designed to be clicked on. They lead directly to your shop without the person having to jump through hoops. The users on Pinterest are also more primed to make purchases. This is why we recommend Pinterest over Instagram.

Overall, Instagram is great for building brand awareness (think influencers), but don't expect much in the way of direct sales from the platform. If you choose to use Instagram, focus more on building your brand and showing off your personality by sharing quotes, stories, and personal photos. There are plenty of Etsy shop owners who've had great success on Instagram, so if that's your thing, then go for it!

There's no right or wrong here. Simply decide and do. Any platform can work for you if used effectively for your niche. Just prioritize consistent and focused effort and you'll be well on your way to six-figure marketing.

CHAPTER 11

Emails That Make $$$

Email marketing is key to any successful business. If you want to build a six-figure Etsy shop, you'll need to build an email list. Period.

Why? Because your email list is completely yours. The way in which you choose to communicate with your subscribers is entirely up to you. You don't have to worry about keywords, algorithms, or SEO.

While a sudden Google algorithm change could drastically drop search engine traffic to your shop, your email list will still be safe. Even if Facebook and Pinterest both disappeared in one day, you would still have the ability to communicate with your customers and make sales.

You are the owner of your email list and no one can take that away from you. It's a guaranteed form of direct contact with your customer base. This is why it's crucial in this day and age for every business to have an email list.

How to Start an Email List

Let's start with the basics. First, you'll need an email marketing platform that allows you to collect email addresses and send out emails.

Our top recommendation is ConvertKit. This is the platform we personally use for all of our businesses and it's served us very well over the years. They have a ton of easy-to-use and very effective features that make email marketing a breeze. They also have excellent and very responsive customer support (a must for us!) plus live classes, tutorials, and workshops for making the most of your email marketing efforts.

Another popular option is MailChimp. We used MailChimp when we were first starting out but felt that it didn't offer all of the features we were looking for. We also had some mixed experiences with their customer support. This is why we switched to ConvertKit and have been with them ever since.

That being said, many Etsy shop owners love MailChimp and report positive experiences with them. MailChimp has come a long way since we first tried them out back in 2016 and now offers many of the same features that ConvertKit does. In the end, you really can't go wrong with either one.

MailChimp is also currently the only email marketing platform that integrates directly with Pattern by Etsy, so if you're planning on having a Pattern site (more on this later), then this could be a distinct advantage as well.

Both ConvertKit and MailChimp have free plans, so you can get started right away. However, the free plans have fewer capabilities and a limited amount of subscribers, so plan to upgrade as you grow your list.

Trust us—a good email marketing platform will more than pay for itself. You'll find that as your subscriber list grows, so do your sales. A reliable way to communicate with your customers through email is essential to a successful shop.

Since ConvertKit is the email marketing platform that we're most familiar with, the rest of this chapter will be written using tools and terminology from ConvertKit. If you're using MailChimp or another platform instead, you can simply adapt our guidelines so they pertain to your specific platform. Most email marketing platforms have similar features, so the same general principles and steps will apply regardless.

Once you've decided on an email marketing platform, just sign up and we'll start growing your list!

How to Grow Your Email List

You'll want to grow your email list over time to include both potential and existing customers. The more ENGAGED subscribers you have, the more effective your marketing efforts will be. We'll talk more about engaged versus cold subscribers later on.

Before we get started, do NOT under any circumstances, pull customer email addresses directly from Etsy. This is against both Etsy's seller agreement and many local laws.

Customers have to explicitly opt in to your email list by voluntarily signing up for it. Trying to collect email addresses in any other way will result in a large volume of unsubscribes and a generally shady reputation for your business. Just don't do it.

Landing Pages and Forms

The easiest way to collect email addresses for your list is to create forms or landing pages that allow customers to sign up, or opt in, to your email list. In ConvertKit, you'll find "Landing Pages & Forms" in the "Grow" tab.

A form is added to an already existing website, while a landing page is a standalone webpage. In both cases, customers simply submit their information (usually first name and email address) and they'll be automatically added to your email list.

If you have a blog or website, you can embed a form onto any page to collect email addresses. ConvertKit has a variety of forms to choose from that you can customize with your shop's branding and colors. Once you publish the form, you can copy the JavaScript or HTML code and add it to your site.

If that all sounded like gibberish to you, don't worry. ConvertKit also offers a ton of landing pages for you to choose from. With a landing page, there's no need for a blog or website. It's simply a standalone webpage, hosted by ConvertKit, that allows customers to opt in to your email list. Easy-peasy.

Once you create your landing page, just hit publish and you'll receive a link to the webpage that you can share everywhere. And we do mean EVERYWHERE. You should share the link to your landing page on social media, shop announcements, confirmation emails, insert cards and notes, and anywhere else you can think of.

As a reminder, when posting links to opt-in pages on Etsy, be sure you're following Etsy's most recent terms, conditions, and guidelines by consulting the Seller Handbook.

Incentives for Joining

Although some customers might join your list simply because they love your shop, most will need an incentive to join.

An incentive is simply a compelling reason for them to subscribe. This would typically be a coupon (e.g., a 15% off coupon for signing up) or a digital freebie (e.g., a free crochet pattern that they can download). Be sure that your landing page or form clearly states which incentive the subscriber will receive by signing up.

If you choose to do a freebie, it should be a free gift that relates to your niche but is NOT available for purchase in your shop. This gift should be digital (i.e., not something you have to mail) that can be easily delivered through email upon sign-up.

For example, if you sell sterling silver jewelry, a good incentive for joining your email list could be a PDF guide on how to clean and care for your silver jewelry.

You can deliver your incentive (coupon or freebie) to new subscribers automatically upon sign-up by creating a welcome sequence. We'll discuss this in the next section.

Your First 1,000 Subscribers

Your initial goal should be to grow your list to at least 1,000 subscribers. This is typically the number where you'll start seeing significant sales from your email marketing efforts.

While this may seem far away when you're just beginning, it won't take too long to reach if you're offering the right opt-in incentives for your ideal customer.

Think about what your ideal customer would be MOST excited to receive from you upon sign-up. If you sell products for babies, for example, then a PDF with 12 little-known tips for caring for a newborn could be a great opt-in.

Our advice is to create two to five different incentives and test them out to see which one is most effective. You should create a different landing page or form for each incentive and then look at the conversion rate for each one. The conversion rate is the percentage of visitors to your landing page who signed up for your email list.

ConvertKit shows conversion rates in the "Landing Pages and Forms" tab. Under the landing page's name, you'll see the number of visitors, number of subscribers, and conversion rate. The higher the conversion rate, the more effective the form is at incentivizing your ideal customers to subscribe.

Try this out with different freebies and coupons to see what works best. For coupons, we recommend a discount of 10% to start, but you can also test out a discount of 15% or more and see if this drastically increases your conversion rate. You can also try out different types of coupons like $10 off or free shipping.

Don't be afraid to play around with and test different freebies and coupons to see what resonates most with your customers. You can also test out different landing page styles, colors, and copy to see if that has any effect on your conversion rates as well.

After a few months of testing, you'll be able to identify the incentives and landing pages that convert the best for your audience. Keep in mind that a certain incentive might convert better on social media and another could convert better on Etsy. Choose what works best for each platform to supercharge your email list growth.

How to Email Your List

In this section, we'll cover the two types of emails you can send to your list.

Sequences

Sequences allow you to send an automated series of emails to your subscribers. These would typically be sent to new subscribers right after they sign up for your list via a landing page or form.

The amazing thing about sequences is that once you set them up properly, the emails go out to new subscribers automatically without you having to lift a finger!

We recommend setting up what's called a welcome sequence for new subscribers. This is where you'll deliver the incentive that the subscriber was promised when they signed up. Your welcome sequence can be just one email with your coupon or freebie attached or it can be several emails.

It's super important that this is set up properly BEFORE you share forms or landing pages, so your new subscriber receives their coupon or freebie right away.

If you've created multiple incentives with different landing pages, as recommended in the previous section, you'll need to set up a separate welcome sequence for each one. The emails can be exactly the same but with different incentives attached.

Just make sure you've set up the proper tags, rules, and automations, so the correct welcome sequences go to the right people. Be sure to set up a different tag for each landing page, so your account shows which subscriber signed up for what incentive.

If you're using ConvertKit, you can learn about sequences, tags, rules, and automations by searching for tutorials or watching their extremely helpful Lunch & Learn video series.

This video series is how we initially got started with ConvertKit. It may seem like a lot at first, but soon enough, you'll be sending sequences and creating automations like a pro!

If you're using MailChimp or another email marketing platform, you'll find similar tutorials for setting these up as well.

Broadcasts

A broadcast is a one-time email that you send to your subscribers. You would typically send these to notify your list about sales, new products, shop updates, or simply to send a regular newsletter. You can send a broadcast manually or schedule it ahead of time. It can be sent to your whole list or just a portion of it.

The vast majority, if not all, of the emails you send to subscribers after the initial welcome sequence will be broadcasts.

Six-Figure Emails

Up to this point, you've learned how to grow your list and the types of emails you can send. Now, it's time to write your first email!

We recommend emailing your list about two to four times per month on average. This is the right balance between establishing a consistent presence in your subscribers' inboxes without overwhelming them with too many emails. The exception to this is during big sales (e.g., Black Friday) or the holiday season, when you may need an extra push to stand out in busy inboxes.

One of the biggest struggles with email is figuring out what to write. It can feel weird and impersonal at first, like you're writing to a bunch of strangers. We totally understand this feeling, but just remember that your email list isn't a bunch of random people. They're potential and existing ideal customers who voluntarily signed up for your email list because they want to hear from YOU. They want updates and news about your shop and products.

Your emails should show off your unique personality, style, and brand. Your customers don't want just another boring "Here's a sale" or "Here's my latest product" email in their inbox. They get dozens of these from other businesses every single day.

Instead, you want your emails to be something your customers actually look forward to reading because they know they'll receive value in every single one. You want your emails to stand out above the others and make sales each and every time, so you can build toward your six-figure empire.

The reality is the size of your email list doesn't matter nearly as much as the number of customers who engage with your emails. Your goal with every email is to guide your customers through the journey of opening the email, reading it, clicking through, and making a purchase. If you've accomplished this, you've written what we call a "Six-Figure Email."

Anatomy of a Six-Figure Email

[Compelling Subject Line]

Hi [Subscriber's First Name],

[First Paragraph: Share a Personal Anecdote]

[Second Paragraph: Apply the Anecdote to Your Ideal Customer]

[Third Paragraph: Make the Sale]

[Sign Off]

[Signature]

[PS]

Breakdown of a Six-Figure Email

1. It starts with a compelling subject line that entices your ideal customer to open the email. Don't just put generic things like "Big Sale" or "10% Off." Emails like this come across as spammy or generic and have a tendency to get lost in inboxes. Try instead to come up with creative subject lines that draw your customers in, while still being relevant to the content of your email. For example, "Guess what I just made for you!" is much more enticing and personal than "New Product On Sale Now."

2. Greet the customer by their first name in your email. You never want your email to start with a generic "Hey you." It takes just a few minutes to set up your emails to automatically populate with subscribers' first names. To do this, you will generally need a short code or tag that you can find through your email marketing platform's help center.

3. The first paragraph should be a quick personal anecdote that draws the reader in and helps them get to know you. You want your customers to look forward to receiving your emails because they feel like an update from a personal friend, as opposed to another detached and faceless business email. Just be sure to keep this section short, so you don't lose their attention before you have a chance to make the sale. This paragraph should be 2–3 sentences at the most.

4. The second paragraph should connect your personal anecdote with your ideal customer's wants or needs. There should be a clear progression between paragraphs one and two that feels natural and makes sense. Keep in mind the basic marketing principle of staying customer focused in this section.

5. Create a natural lead-in between the first two paragraphs and the item you're selling, the sale you're announcing, or the coupon you're offering. While you never want your emails to appear too salesy, you should still make clear what you're selling or offering in this section. Be sure that your sales copy directly relates to your first two paragraphs, so it doesn't sound random or forced. There should be a clear flow and sense of continuity throughout your entire email.

6. Add a 1–2-sentence sign-off, so the email doesn't end abruptly. You can wish the customer a great weekend, finish with a fun quote, or anything else that feels right.

7. Sign your first name and include a small thumbnail-sized photo of yourself. Again, this adds a personal touch and helps customers put a face to your name. Also include your shop name and URL underneath your signature.

8. Add a PS (postscript) to the bottom with a one-sentence summary of the email's content, highlighting the sale, item, or coupon you're promoting. Many customers don't read emails in full and simply scroll to the bottom. You'll want to capture their attention by adding your call to action in the PS one final time.

9. In addition to the text, you should also add relevant product photos to your email. Most items sold on Etsy are very visual, so a photo in and of itself is an enticing way to lead customers to your shop. Be sure to make your photos clickable by adding a hyperlink that leads directly to your listing.

Example of a Six-Figure Email

Subject: I want you to feel special!

Hi [Customer Name],

My son, Ben, was SO excited when he came home from school yesterday! His teacher had given every member of his 2nd-grade class a special award just for being awesome. How sweet is that?

(Note: You can add a photo of Ben with his award here. It's not necessary but can be a good personal touch.)

This was an important reminder that we ALL deserve to feel special. It sounds a bit cheesy, but I personally believe that, even as adults, we still get that warm and fuzzy feeling, whenever we're reminded of our unique brand of awesomeness. Don't you?

So, I wanted to share that special feeling with you today by offering you an exclusive 20% DISCOUNT on anything in my shop, just for being YOU. I truly appreciate your being here and supporting Rose Gold Shop [link to your shop].

Use the coupon code SPECIAL at checkout for a 20% discount on anything in my Etsy shop [link to your shop] until tomorrow (7/13) ONLY at 11:59 p.m. ET.

(Note: You should add your product or shop photo here. Make sure it's clickable with a link to your listing or shop.)

I'll talk to you soon! Until then, thanks again for being you.

Love,

[Thumbnail Photo]

Emily

Rose Gold Shop

etsy.com/shop/rosegoldshop

PS Don't forget to use the code SPECIAL at checkout for 20% off anything in my Etsy shop [link] until 7/13 at 11:59 p.m. ET!

Congrats! You now have all the tools needed to write powerful marketing emails that SELL, while still offering a personal touch that keeps customers coming back for more. This one profitable skill alone can result in a high-performing Etsy shop that generates hundreds of thousands of dollars in sales each year.

Tips for Writing Six-Figure Emails

- A Six-Figure Email has two main goals: (1) to build and nurture an ongoing relationship with your customer and (2) to encourage the customer to visit your shop and make a purchase. Both goals work synergistically and a strong marketing email has a balance between the two.

- You never want customers to get the sense that the only reason you're emailing them is to take their money. Nobody likes the feeling of being sold to. Instead, focus on building a connection and the sales will follow.

- While you want your emails to be personal, they should still be short and to the point. Your customers are busy and don't have time to read a long multipage email. Each paragraph should be only 2–3 sentences at the most to ensure the email holds your customer's attention all the way through.

- Every sentence should be compelling enough to draw your customer into reading the next sentence and so on. Your goal is for customers to read the entire email, as those who do are the most likely to make a purchase.

- Just like with social media, you never want to simply chase the one-time sale. Email marketing is about developing relationships with your customers. Your goal with each email is to foster a loyal customer base that buys from you over and over again.

- You want your customers to get to know you and see you as a real person, not just another faceless business. Even if a customer doesn't buy from this email or the next one, as long as they stay on your list and keep reading your emails, they are very likely to buy from you in the future. Remember that a six-figure business is built from a large volume of consistent sales over time.

Unsubscribes

Even if you follow everything in this chapter to a tee, you will inevitably have some people who unsubscribe from your email list.

Don't be afraid of unsubscribes—those aren't your people anyway. Let them go and make room for new subscribers who are more aligned with what you have to offer.

Always stay true to who you are and what your shop represents. As long as your emails are valuable and you're not flooding your list with too many at a time, your ideal customer will happily stay on as part of your tribe.

There may even be circumstances where you WANT certain groups of people on your list to unsubscribe. We'll discuss that next.

Engaged vs Cold Subscribers

We mentioned earlier in the chapter that 1,000 subscribers is a good starting goal for seeing optimal returns from your marketing efforts.

While this still holds true, the overall number of subscribers on your list is not as important as the number of ENGAGED subscribers. Engaged subscribers are the ones on your list who actually open or click on your emails.

If you have 1,000 email subscribers but only 1% of them open your emails, that's only 10 people who you've actually reached with your marketing efforts. That's not going to result in many sales for your shop, if any at all.

But if you have 1,000 email subscribers and 25% of them open your emails, that's 250 people. You'll receive far more sales with that.

The more engaged subscribers you have, the more sales you'll make. This is why your average open rate (the percentage of subscribers who open your email) is at least as important as the number of subscribers you have.

You can see both the open and click rate (the percentage of subscribers who clicked through to your shop) for each of your sequences and broadcasts in ConvertKit. A good open rate for email is between 17–28%, while a good click-through rate is between 2–8%.

You should keep a close eye on these rates and make adjustments as needed. They will help you determine which subject lines and types of emails result in the highest amount of engagement from your list. Do more of what works and less of what doesn't to increase your number of engaged subscribers.

Conversely, a subscriber who isn't opening your emails is not helping your shop. This is called a cold or inactive subscriber. A cold subscriber is anyone on your list who hasn't opened or clicked on an email from you in the last 90 days.

You're not making any sales from these subscribers and they could even be costing you money if your email marketing platform charges by the number of subscribers.

Worse yet, cold subscribers hurt your open and click rates, which drastically decreases your sender reputation with Gmail and other email service providers. This results in a higher percentage of your emails ending up in junk, spam, or promotions causing a vicious cycle that leads to even fewer people seeing and opening your emails.

The best way to avoid this is to periodically (every 6 months or so) identify and clean cold subscribers off your list. To do this, you would send your cold subscribers at least one email (we sometimes send out 2 or 3) asking if they want to remain on your list. If they don't click on the link after a week, you should delete them. You can find the exact step-by-step process for identifying and deleting cold subscribers under "How to Prune Cold Subscribers from Your List" in ConvertKit's Help Center.

While it might be hard to delete subscribers, just remember that the cold ones aren't helping you in any way. In fact, they're hurting your open rates, putting your sender reputation at risk, and costing you money. By cutting them loose, you're effectively making room for new subscribers who will actually open your emails and buy from you.

Pro Tips

Here are a few final must-know email marketing tips:

- Try to avoid sending emails from a Gmail address. It looks unprofessional and can often be marked as spam. We recommend investing in a domain (more on this later), so you can set up a personalized email, such as emily@rosegoldshop.com. That being said, if you're new to this and an @gmail.com account is all you have right now, don't let that stop you from getting started with email marketing right away. Sending emails from a Gmail address is still way better than not sending emails at all.

- Customers will typically see the name of the email sender in their inbox, as opposed to the email address. You can set up your sender name in your email marketing platform. We recommend using your first name plus your shop name (e.g., Emily at Rose Gold Shop or Emily | Rose Gold Shop) so customers can easily identify who you are.

- Every marketing email must have a valid physical address at the bottom. This is the law and can't be avoided. If your business doesn't have a physical address, we recommend getting a small PO box at your local post office and using the address for that in the footer of your email. Another great advantage of ConvertKit is that they're set up to legally allow current customers to use their physical address for free. That address is automatically added to the footer of every email, so it's hassle-free!

- Every email needs an unsubscribe link at the bottom of it. Like having a physical address, this is required by law. This link needs to be clearly visible and not hidden in any way.

CHAPTER 12

Profitable Ads

Paid advertising has the ability to skyrocket your sales by putting your products in front of ideal customers, who might never have heard of your shop otherwise. This drastically expands your reach, customer base, and profit potential.

When used effectively, paid advertising works synergistically with social media and email marketing. The ads bring in new customers, who can then join your Facebook Group and subscriber list. They become a part of your tribe with the potential to turn into superfans and repeat buyers. In this case, the dollars spent on an ad don't just result in one sale but possibly many sales down the line.

While the idea of paying for ads might sound a bit daunting, especially when you're first starting out, trust us when we say it's definitely worth it. In business, you need to spend money to make money. This includes advertising.

Think about all the big successful companies out there. The one thing that Apple, Coca-Cola, and Disney have in common is that they all pay for advertising.

Don't think of advertising as a cost but, rather, an investment that will return to you multiple times over. When you spend money on ads, you'll significantly expand your customer base and increase monthly sales. This means MORE five-star reviews, social media followers, email opt-ins, word of mouth, and repeat customers leading to exponentially more money for your business in the long run than what you initially spent on the ad.

And the best part? Paid ads cost a lot less than you'd probably expect. In fact, you can start running Etsy ads for as little as $1 a day. That's less than the price of a latte from Starbucks.

As you'll learn in this chapter, the dollar amount you spend on ads is far less important than having a solid strategy for how your ad budget is spent. We'll teach you exactly how to get the best bang for your advertising buck, so you can grow your shop quickly and worry-free.

Onsite Ads

Onsite ads, also known as Etsy Ads, are shown directly on the Etsy platform. They are typically displayed within search results but can also show up on category pages, in the "You May Also Like" section, and in other locations throughout the platform.

Etsy Ads give a listing that you've chosen a higher or more prominent placement on their site. Their purpose is to get a specific listing of yours in front of more potential customers.

For example, if your listing is organically ranked on the bottom of page five in search results for a particular keyword, Etsy Ads might make this listing appear on the top of page two instead. This can result in a huge boost in sales, especially if your ad shows up on the top of page one for a popular keyword.

With Etsy Ads, you only pay when someone clicks on your ad. In most cases, you can expect to pay $0.20 to $0.30 per click, depending on how competitive your keywords are.

This section focuses primarily on the best strategy for increasing sales using onsite Etsy Ads. If you need help setting them up first, look for "How to Set Up and Manage an Etsy Ads Campaign" in the Etsy Help Center.

In order to get the best results, you'll first need to understand how ad placement is determined. Etsy Ads work through an auction system, where your listings compete against others for an ad spot.

The main factors that affect your listing's performance in the auction are listing quality, bid amount (how much you're willing to pay per click), likelihood of sales (factors about the shopper, such as time of day and the device their using), and relevance to the search query.

Some factors, such as likelihood of sales, are out of your hands, while others are very much in your control, namely, listing quality. While your listing quality score is not disclosed by Etsy, they have shared that it's largely based on clicks, views, favorites, and purchases.

Etsy also specifically states on its site that "if a listing has a low quality score it may need a higher bid to receive competitive placement." This means the reverse also applies. If you want to pay less per click, your listing quality score needs to be high.

In the end, Etsy's goal is to feature listings on the first page that relevant buyers are most likely to click on and purchase. If you want first- or second-page placement for your onsite ad, then you'll need to choose a listing that's already proven to sell.

In other words, you should choose your highest-converting listings for onsite ads. While it may be tempting to run ads for listings that aren't selling as well, the principle behind a successful Etsy Ad is to supercharge what's already working for you.

To check conversion rates for your listings, go to "Stats" inside the Shop Manager. Click on "Orders" and then calculate the conversion rates of your best-selling products (# of views/# of orders). Set up advertising for your highest converting listings (we recommend 5–10 to start) and then let them sit for 30 days, so the algorithm can collect data.

After 30 days, check your performance graphs under Etsy Ads to see how your ads are doing. Then, you can make adjustments accordingly to increase performance:

- If your ad has high views and low clicks, you should change the main photo. It's likely not eye-catching enough or not relevant to the customer you're trying to reach.

- If your ad has high clicks and low sales, you should adjust the details within the listing, such as the remaining photos or description. You can also tweak the pricing.

- If your ad has low views and low clicks, you've likely chosen a listing with a low quality score. You should consider no longer advertising this particular listing, so higher quality ones can receive more budget. Another option is to return to chapter 4 of this book and improve your listing before promoting it again.

- If your ad has high views and high clicks, this is where you want to be! Keep running the ad and increase your budget as needed.

Here are some additional tips for running effective and profitable Etsy ads:

- *Don't start running ads until you've completed the other steps in this book.* If you haven't properly set up and optimized your shop for success, paid advertising won't be very effective for you. You'll save yourself both time and money in the long run by going through Steps 1–3 first and ensuring your shop is the best it can be before you pay for ads. Also be sure to set up your social media and email marketing so you don't miss out on the opportunity to nurture new customers into repeat buyers.

- *Start small.* Don't feel that you need to jump to the maximum budget of $25 a day right off the bat. In fact, we strongly advise that you DON'T do this. Start with just $1–$5 a day and keep a close eye on your stats. A higher budget won't result in more sales if you don't know how to run an effective ad yet. Once you have an ad that's making consistent sales, then you can incrementally increase your budget for that ad.

- *Keep an eye on your stats.* You should never run your ads on autopilot. Always keep a close eye on them and tweak them as needed. If an ad is performing well, increase its budget. If an ad isn't performing well, stop running the ad and put that money into an ad that's performing better. By doing this, you'll receive more bang for your buck without having to increase your overall ad spend.

Offsite Ads

Offsite Ads is a separate program run by Etsy that displays ads for your products on other platforms, such as Google, Facebook, Bing, Instagram, and Pinterest.

The cool thing about Offsite Ads is that there's no up-front cost. You only pay an ad fee when your product is sold.

When a product sale is made from an Offsite Ad, Etsy charges a fee that is a percentage of the sale price. For example, if a $100 product is sold through Offsite Ads and Etsy takes a 15% advertising fee, that would be $15.

All sellers are automatically enrolled in Offsite Ads. If you made $10,000 or more on Etsy in the past year, you are required to participate in the program and will get a discounted advertising fee of 12%. If you made less than $10,000 on Etsy in the past year, participation is optional and the advertising fee is 15%.

Even if you're new to Etsy or have made less than $10,000 in the last year, we still recommend that you stay enrolled in the program. The rate of return tends to be higher with Offsite Ads than Etsy Ads because you're reaching a wider audience. This means more potential customers for your shop and more people joining your email list and Facebook Group, so you can keep those sales coming in.

As always, our strategy here is to expand our customer base, so we can create loyal fans which result in repeat business. With this in mind, Offsite Ads don't just result in one-time sales but potentially many sales in the future, increasing our bottom line even further.

Similar to Etsy Ads, the best thing you can do to ensure high-performing Offsite Ads is to maintain high-quality listings using the strategies discussed in chapter 4. Listings are advertised in the Offsite Ads program based on what performs the best on each platform. A listing with a high quality score has an increased chance of being advertised.

Most of the offsite platforms also have their own criteria for listings that are advertised on their websites. You can improve the chances of your ad being featured on a specific platform by matching their criteria. You can learn more about these criteria in the Etsy Help Center under "How Etsy's Offsite Ads Work".

Your goal is to have as many of your listings as possible featured in the Offsite Ads program. While you don't have any input on which listings are chosen or what platform they will be shown on, you can drastically improve your chances of participation on high-traffic sites by making sure every listing in your shop is top-notch. This means eye-catching photos, strong keywords, and an effective title.

This is why strong listings should always be your top priority on Etsy. If at any time your ads aren't as effective as you'd like them to be, return to chapter 4 and work to improve your listings. In the end, a strong foundation is always the best way to increase sales.

CHAPTER 13

3 Tips to 3x Your Sales

In addition to social media, email marketing, and paid ads, there are some additional tools on the Etsy platform that can drastically increase your sales for free.

These powerful tools are super easy to set up and often underutilized by shop owners. You'll find all three of these in the Shop Manager under Marketing -> Sales and Discounts.

At the end of this chapter, we'll offer a bonus tip that will ramp up your sales even more. Let's dive in!

Tip #1: Sales

A sale allows you to set lower prices for your whole shop or just a few items over a fixed period of time. The discounted prices will be available to anyone who visits your shop without the need for a special code. Sales can run for up to 30 days.

Sales can often lead to higher conversion rates, which can boost your rankings in Etsy search results. This can lead to MORE revenue across the board during the duration of your sale, which is a huge win!

In general, sales should be 10% off a specific group of items. Since anyone can access them, sales typically don't need to be advertised. The only exception is special sales offering a deeper discount (i.e., 25% off for Black Friday) or last-chance sales for items you're planning to retire that aren't selling well (i.e., 40–50% off).

In addition to offering a percentage off, you can also offer free shipping as a sale. We recommend setting an order minimum for this. For example, if a customer buys two or more items from your shop, they'll receive free shipping OR if a customer spends $50 or more in your shop, they'll receive free shipping. This encourages buyers to place larger orders.

Tip #2: Promo Codes

Promo codes are basically just digital coupons. They're different from sales in that the discounted pricing is only available to customers who have the promo code.

For promo codes, you can offer a percentage off (e.g., 20% off), fixed amount off (e.g., $5 off), or free shipping. Similar to sales, you can require an order minimum of a certain amount of items (e.g., 2 or more items) or an order total (e.g., spend $50 or more), in order for the customer to qualify for the offer.

Promo codes are a great way to encourage increased sales from your Facebook Group, email list, and other social media platforms. You can even add a promo code to your package insert cards alongside your review ask. Your promo codes should be a deeper discount than your sales.

Sales should typically be 10% off because the discounts are available to everyone. Promo codes, on the other hand, are special discounts for your most loyal customers. This is why we recommend promo codes that are 15% off or more.

Promo codes are also a great way to make customers in your Facebook Group and email list feel like VIPs. After all, these are your loyal fans and repeat buyers. They deserve a little something extra every now and then!

Pro Tip: DON'T share the same promo code in your Facebook Group and email list at the same time. Mix it up and offer different promo codes at different times so customers have an incentive to join both.

Tip #3: Targeted Offers

Targeted offers send automatic discounts via email to specific groups of shoppers. Like promo codes, these offers can be a percentage off, fixed amount off, or free shipping.

The "Thank You" offer sends a promo code to customers after their orders ship. This offer gives them a discount on their next order from your shop.

The "Abandoned Cart" offer sends a promo code to people who leave an item from your shop in their cart without checking out. This offer incentivizes shoppers who may be on the fence to complete their purchase.

The "Favorited Item" offer sends a promo code to those who have favorited an item from your shop. This offer puts your item front and center, so it stands out against other similar items they might have favorited.

All three of these offers work very well and we recommend using all of them in your shop. We've found that offering a 15% discount for each of these works the best.

Bonus Tip: Stats and Analytics

If you want to increase sales in your shop, keeping a close eye on your stats is absolutely essential. These stats are an objective measure of what's working well for you and what needs improvement. As always, do more of what works and tweak or eliminate what doesn't.

To see your stats in Etsy, go to Shop Manager -> Stats. At the top, you can see the number of shop visits, orders, conversion rate, and revenue.

This allows you to track how your shop is doing and whether your efforts are paying off. You should see a steady increase in all of these metrics as you implement the steps in this book.

We recommend looking at your stats for ranges of 30, 90, and 365 days to get the best bird's-eye view of how your shop is performing. Don't be alarmed by day-to-day fluctuations in these metrics. This happens all the time and can be attributed to completely random factors. Keep your focus on the big picture.

Below the top graph, you can see how shoppers found you. These stats are an essential measure of how well your keywords, SEO, social media, and ads are working for you. Keep a close eye on these to see what's working best and what needs improvement, so you can maximize your shop traffic from all sources. If your social media channels are new, give them at least 60–90 days to pick up momentum before evaluating these stats.

Finally, you can see how individual listings are performing at the bottom. This allows you to identify your best-selling products and least-selling products.

If a listing isn't performing as well as you'd expected and it's been at least 30 days since it's been up, consider changing the main photo, trying different keywords, or tweaking the title/description. If after several rounds of changes, the listing still isn't performing well, consider retiring the product by offering a last-chance sale at 40–50% off.

If a listing is performing well, don't change a thing. Instead, run Etsy Ads for it, so it can reach a wider audience.

We also recommend that you install Google Analytics for your shop, as it shows many useful stats that Etsy does not. This is a free web analytics service offered by Google that tracks and reports website traffic allowing you to get a better idea of who is visiting your shop. To set up Google Analytics, visit the "Web Analytics" page in the Etsy Help Center.

Finally, do your best not to get emotional about these stats. It can be disappointing if a listing, ad, or social media platform doesn't perform as well as you'd hoped. Just keep a level head and figure out how to improve it. This isn't a personal failing—it's just analyzing how to make your business better. Oftentimes, a disappointing stat can be majorly improved with just a few simple tweaks. This is why checking stats regularly is so important.

In the end, remember that Etsy wants you to make as many sales as possible in your shop. More money for you also means more money for them. This is why you should take advantage of all the marketing tools they're offering you for free. More times than not, they can have a high impact for the least amount of effort.

STEP FIVE: SCALE

Congrats! You've successfully launched, optimized, and grown your profitable Etsy shop. Now, it's time to scale it into a thriving business.

This step is all about legitimizing and scaling your business. You'll learn about incorporating, filing taxes, and outsourcing, so you can have a professional and growing presence in the business world.

You're well on your way to being official CEO of your very own Etsy empire. Let's get to it!

CHAPTER 14

Let's Talk Business

In this chapter, we'll talk about LLCs, S corps, accounting, establishing a business presence, and more.

If that all sounds a bit scary and overwhelming, you're not alone! We're actually a bit embarrassed to admit that we avoided establishing an LLC for the first year and a half of running our businesses because we thought it would be too much of a headache.

As it turns out, setting it up was SO much easier than we thought and well worth it. So, don't be afraid to just dive in on this. It's an exciting first step toward an official six-figure business.

A quick caveat before we dive deeper into business talk: We're not lawyers, accountants, or legal experts of any kind. You should always consult a professional before making any legal or tax-related decisions for your business.

While this section teaches you some basics, every business is different and has unique needs. Only a tax or legal professional who is familiar with your shop can give you the right answers. Many business laws vary from state to state, so always do your research first.

We have an amazing accountant who helps with all our businesses, and we'd honestly be a mess without him. Oftentimes, consulting a professional isn't as big an expense as you might think. When we started our first business (a food blog), we made just $12,000 in our first year. Our accountant only charged us $60 for filing our taxes and we ended up with a huge tax refund that we might not have gotten otherwise.

So, do yourself a favor and consult a professional as early as possible. It pays off in the long run.

How to Succeed in Business (With an LLC)

If you're serious about turning your Etsy dream into a business, you should highly consider forming a limited liability company, also known as an LLC.

An LLC offers many benefits that will protect your business and help it grow faster. Even better, it gives you a sense of pride and professionalism knowing that your business is official.

The primary purpose of an LLC is to maintain a legal separation between your personal and business assets. This means that if your business gets sued, your personal assets shouldn't be at risk. While the chance of your business being sued is incredibly slim, this is still a smart precaution to have in place. Think of it as insurance for your personal assets.

In addition to legal protection, you'll experience financial benefits from an LLC, as well. Once you form your LLC, you'll be given an Employer Identification Number (EIN), which enables you to open a business bank account. This allows you to apply for business credit cards, which often have better rewards than personal ones.

We recommend that you utilize your business bank account and credit cards SOLELY for business purposes. If you buy so much as a pencil for your business, charge it to your business credit card, so you can keep track of your expenses. The separation between your business and personal accounts will be a huge help come tax season.

You can also use your EIN to apply for a sales tax resale certificate, which gives you access to tax-free wholesale prices on your supplies. This can significantly reduce your costs and result in a higher profit margin per item. This means more revenue for your business!

Setting up an LLC is much easier and less expensive than you might think. In most states, you can set up and maintain an LLC for $100 to $300 a year. This amount is definitely worth the peace of mind and can be made up with the discounts and tax breaks you may receive on wholesale supplies.

Here's the basic step-by-step process for setting up an LLC. This process can vary a bit by state, so make sure you do your own research and consult a professional whenever necessary.

1. *Choose a name for your LLC.* Make sure the name is available and fits within the naming guidelines for your state. If your LLC is a different name than your Etsy shop, you will also need a doing business as (DBA) that is your shop name (this is a simple process that just requires an additional form).

2. *Choose a resident agent in your state.* Most states require a resident agent when forming an LLC. This is a person or business entity that accepts tax and legal documents on behalf of your business.

3. *File the articles of organization with your state.* This is a simple form that you fill out and mail to the designated department within your state along with any associated fees. They are also sometimes called articles of incorporation.

That's it! While you'll have to research the exact details that apply to your state, this is the general process for filing an LLC. It's pretty simple and will save you a lot in the long run.

One last thing to consider is whether or not you want to file your taxes as an S corporation (S corp). This is basically an IRS tax status that you can choose to file under as an LLC. The main advantage of an S corp is that it allows business owners to be treated as employees for tax purposes. This can save you money on taxes, but is a bit more complicated and will likely require an accountant. The general consensus is that if you can pay yourself a salary of at least $10,000 in distributions a year as a business owner, then S corp status could be beneficial.

You can start with just an LLC first and then consult an accountant when you're ready to file as an S corp.

Taxes and Accounting

Tax season can be a major headache for many small business owners, but it doesn't have to be. You just need to stay organized and track your expenses throughout the year. Many small businesses need to file estimated quarterly taxes, so staying on top of your taxes all year is the smart and advisable thing to do.

As we mentioned before, having a business bank account and credit card that you only use for business purposes will help you stay organized. Always keep your personal and business assets separate right from the beginning and you'll save yourself a lot of trouble when you're filing.

We like to keep track of our expenses and profits in an Excel sheet. Every time we purchase something for our business, whether it's an item or a service, we record it in the Excel sheet. We also track our profits there too.

Each month, we calculate our net profit by subtracting expenses from our earnings. This number is how much we made in our business for that particular month. You should keep track of quarterly and yearly expenses too.

The accounting process will vary depending on how complex your business is. It can be helpful to invest in tax software, such as TurboTax or H&R Block, especially if you're not using an accountant. If you have employees or contractors, you may need payroll software as well.

We want to avoid going into too much detail in this section because every business is different. The way taxes and accounting work for our businesses will likely be very different from yours.

The key takeaway here is that you need a system for tracking expenses and profits throughout the year. Do NOT wait until filing time to figure it all out. You'll be overwhelmed and far less accurate in your estimations.

What's Your Mission?

Now that your business is official, you need a mission statement. This might sound corny, but it's important to be able to articulate what you do and who your business is for.

This is similar to when we discussed branding in chapter 1 but with a bit more detail. It's basically a short summary of your company's purpose.

Your mission statement should be an action-based statement that answers these questions:

- What is the purpose of your business?
- How do you serve your customers?
- What makes your business unique?

For inspiration, search for the mission statements of other businesses that you admire. Many of them have this posted on their website or publicly available elsewhere.

Write your mission statement down and keep it somewhere easily accessible. You should read through it every so often as a reminder of why your business matters and the important role it plays in the lives of your customers.

This sense of purpose will provide motivation and the drive to push forward whenever things feel hard. It will keep your business on track and guide it toward its full potential.

Business Cards

In the Internet age, business cards are becoming less common, but we still firmly believe that every business should have one.

A physical card with your name and shop on it really makes your business feel real. It's also a great way to spread the word about who you are and what you do.

Keep your business cards simple. Just your full name, shop name, URL, and logo. We order the standard business cards from Vistaprint.

We always keep a few business cards in our wallets, just in case. You never know when opportunity might strike.

Website

Every business needs a website. This is your little piece of home on the Internet.

While your Etsy shop does count as a website, you may want to consider having a separate, additional site for your business. This will legitimize your business, help potential customers find you, and serve as your home base. You'll also have more freedom to customize your site with your own branding and style.

You need just two things to start a website: (1) a domain name and (2) web hosting.

As we discussed in chapter 3, a domain name is simply the URL a user types into a browser to access your website (i.e., yourshopname.com). This functions as the physical address for your site and also allows you to set up a personalized email address (i.e., yourname@yourdomainname.com), as discussed in chapter 11.

In addition to your domain name, you'll need hosting. Web hosting is essentially the process of renting space online for your website. You have two main options for this: (1) Pattern by Etsy and (2) a hosting company.

Pattern is a personalized website for your business with hosting services provided through Etsy's platform. It's super easy to set up—all you need is your domain name, which you can purchase on namecheap.com or directly through Etsy.

Once you're all set up, your Etsy shop listings will instantly sync with your Pattern site. From there, you'll manage all your inventory for both Pattern and your shop through the Shop Manager.

Another option is to create your own business site using a hosting company. You can purchase your domain name directly through your hosting service (many even offer the domain name for free with your hosting package). Some inexpensive hosting services include Bluehost and SiteGround.

This option can be a bit more challenging than Pattern, especially if you don't have any web design experience, but allows for complete freedom and customization. If you have a vision for your website, but lack the skills to create it, you can always hire a web designer to bring your ideas to life.

Although a website is important, there are extra costs and work associated with starting and maintaining a website. Before you take this step, make sure your Etsy shop is the best it can be and sales are steadily climbing.

Online Business Presence

In addition to your website, you should also establish a strong online business presence.

You'll start by setting up your business on LinkedIn. Think of this as your virtual business card. You should create a LinkedIn Company Page for your shop, as well as a personal profile showing that you are the owner.

A presence on LinkedIn not only legitimizes your business but also creates the opportunity for networking. You should connect with other business owners in your niche and grow your network. Stay active on this platform to help your business flourish.

You'll also want to claim your business on Google and set up a profile for it. This will give your business more visibility in search results.

Everything discussed in this chapter will support you in building a professional, visible, and sustainable business. You're well on your way!

CHAPTER 15

More $$$ for Less Work

There are two ways to make more money for your business with less work on your part: outsourcing and diversifying.

This chapter is all about outsourcing. We'll talk about diversifying in the next step.

You'll want to consider the strategies discussed here when your Etsy shop has grown to a point where you can no longer single-handedly fulfill all the roles in your business.

Most likely, when you're first starting out, your business will be just you. Although it'll be busy from the get-go, your workload will still be manageable for one person.

But as you grow, you'll experience a drastic increase in customers, orders, and sales. This is great news because it means more profit for your business, but it can also become overwhelming for just one person to handle.

As an Etsy business owner, you wear a lot of hats. You're creating, photographing, copywriting, packaging, shipping, marketing, and so much more. At a certain point, it becomes smarter and more efficient to hire out some of these tasks. If you don't, growth will begin to stall and your business won't be sustainable.

Outsourcing allows your business to make more money with less of your time. While outsourcing is an expense, when done effectively, your profits will drastically increase.

Many of the professionals you would hire are specialists in a specific area (e.g., a photographer specializes in photography) and can provide better results in less time than you could accomplish on your own.

Another reason to outsource is quality control. If you have more responsibilities than you can reasonably handle on your own and you don't hire help, this will inevitably result in a decrease in quality.

If you want a successful business, it is absolutely crucial to maintain quality. Poor production or packaging can result in unhappy customers, negative reviews, and returns. Lack of communication on social media or email can result in losing loyal customers.

It's not worth the risk. Outsource to avoid losing momentum in the business you've worked so hard to grow.

Choosing to outsource aspects of your business to a trusted professional, who provides high-quality work, will give your business a huge boost and result in rising profits, catapulting you into six figures and beyond.

Just think: Where would Amazon or Coca-Cola be today if only one person was working there? A profitable business comes from strength in numbers.

So, if the time is right, don't be afraid to take this next step. It's a huge milestone for your business. When you start to outsource, your profit potential grows exponentially and the sky becomes the limit.

When to Outsource

So now, you're probably wondering, how do I know when it's the right time to outsource?

The answer to this question varies greatly depending on your unique business, other jobs or responsibilities you may have, and your schedule.

If you're working on your Etsy business full-time, you probably won't need to outsource as quickly in order to grow. But if you're only working on your business part-time or simply have a lot of other commitments in your life, you'll probably need to outsource faster.

Outsourcing essentially gives you your time back. It frees up more time for expanding your business, caring for your family, engaging in self-care, traveling, and so much more.

There are two main indicators that it's time to outsource:

1. *You can afford it.* The profits from your shop have exceeded your living expenses and you find yourself with extra money available to invest in your business.
2. *There's not enough time to keep up with the demands of your shop.* Your shop has grown to the point where it's difficult to keep up and ensure quality with just one person.

Other factors include how labor-intensive your products are to make, how difficult they are to package (i.e., fragile items), how many orders are coming in each day, and how fast your business is growing. The key is to take a bird's-eye view of your business, so you can look ahead and begin outsourcing BEFORE you get overwhelmed.

Also, remember that you don't have to outsource multiple tasks at once either. You can start with just one and go from there.

In the end, only you can decide when it's time to outsource. Do so when the timing feels right.

How to Outsource

You'll typically want to outsource the tasks you are the least skilled at or enjoy the least (these will often be the same tasks).

If a specific task takes you five hours to complete, why not hire a professional who can complete it in three hours? If another task makes you want to pull your hair out, why not hire a professional who actually enjoys it?

You can even hire someone to assist you in larger tasks, such as production or shipping, while still working on the same task yourself. This will be faster and more efficient than doing it on your own.

Here are examples of tasks you can outsource and how to outsource each one:

- *Production* – If you're struggling to keep up with orders for handmade items, it might be time to hire a production partner. This is someone who can assist you in making inventory for your Etsy shop. A good place to start is to reach out to an art school or studio in your area that offers classes in the same niche as yours. They may have students (or teachers) who are eager to help!

- *Photography* – If your product photos could use a boost, hiring a photographer is a great way to outsource. Professional photographers are trained to provide higher-quality photos in far less time than it would take for you to photograph and edit on your own. With ten photos needed for each new product listing, hiring a photographer could be a huge time-saver. Higher-quality photos will also result in better rankings and increased sales.

- *Shipping* – If you're having trouble keeping up with shipping and fulfillment, you can consider dropshipping. This may or may not be viable depending on what kind of items you sell. If you're interested in dropshipping, this article will get you started: oberlo.com/blog/etsy-dropshipping. Another option is to simply hire an assistant to help you with shipping-related tasks.

- *Social Media* – If you're having issues keeping up with social media, a social media manager can make your life so much easier. They'll not only manage your social media presence but also grow your channels and hone your strategy resulting in more business for your shop.

- *General Tasks* – If you just need overall help with your business, a virtual assistant can work wonders for you. A virtual assistant is typically an independent contractor who provides remote administrative services for business owners.

You can find many of these professionals on Upwork or through other similar sites. Just make sure you properly vet potential candidates by assessing their qualifications, conducting interviews, and checking references.

Again, outsourcing is just one way for you to scale as you grow. In Step Six, you'll learn how to diversify into a specific type of product that you'll create once and sell repeatedly. This will drastically increase your income with very little additional work.

Once you've mastered both outsourcing and diversifying, you can soar to six figures and beyond with less work and more time for you. From then on, your business will always flow from a place of fun and creativity without the grind.

STEP SIX: SKYROCKET
(to $100K and Beyond!)

This is it! You've made it. You've crossed that six-figure mark and your business just keeps booming.

In this section, we'll teach you the highly coveted secrets of a six-figure business. You'll also learn the number one way to diversify your Etsy shop to make even MORE money with less effort. Finally, we'll share some tips for keeping up the momentum, so you can continue to grow beyond your wildest dreams.

You're well on your way to earning multi-six or even seven figures selling on Etsy. Keep going!

CHAPTER 16

Six-Figure Secrets

Over nearly a decade, we've learned so much about what it takes to successfully grow and scale a business that it's hard to put it all into words.

We've made some mistakes, while also celebrating countless victories over the years. Through research, hard work, and trial and error, we've come a long way from where we started. It's been a wild ride and we're so excited to share all that we've learned with you.

While the previous sections were filled with actionable strategy, tips, and tools to grow your business, this chapter is mostly about mindset— a powerful but often overlooked aspect of running a profitable business.

This chapter could honestly fill an entire book, but for the sake of efficiency, we've condensed it down to our top FIVE most important success secrets for your six-figure Etsy business.

These secrets will transform your mindset to that of a successful business owner, so you can crush your goals and make your first $100,000 even faster. Let's get started!

Secret #1: Go BIG

If you want to be a six-figure business owner, you need to go big from the start. This means owning your prices, knowing your worth, and growing your shop without hesitation.

Many of us have imposter syndrome when it comes to growing our businesses. We don't see ourselves as the successful business leader, so we subconsciously hold ourselves back.

We keep our prices too low because we're afraid nobody will buy. We stall our social media and email growth because we're afraid to show up in front of our customers. We hold ourselves back from our true potential because we're afraid to shine.

This is completely natural and we all experience it from time to time. Just remember that if you want to live the dream, you need to go big, even when it's scary.

If your Etsy shop and income aren't growing as quickly as you want them to, ask yourself:

- Am I subconsciously holding myself back?
- In what ways am I holding myself back?
- How can I go BIGGER?

If you want to make six figures, you need to know your worth and go for it from the very beginning. The more you believe in yourself, the more your ideal customers can feel that and will be excited to purchase from you.

I deserve a six-figure business. I deserve glowing success. I deserve to shine. Repeat these statements to yourself daily until you truly believe them.

Secret #2: Stay True to Yourself

Your business is a representation of who you are. Always be authentically and unapologetically YOU.

Etsy is the platform for selling unique handmade items, which means no other seller on Etsy offers exactly what you do. This isn't another big box site with twenty sellers peddling the exact same thing. Your items are unique and your brand is unique. Own that.

If there's anything all six-figure businesses have in common, it's that they're not afraid to showcase who they're for. Never try to fit into a box. Never try to sell to everyone. Focus on your ideal customers and tap into how who you are can make their lives better.

If negative reviews or unsubscribes get you down, just remind yourself that those aren't your people. Listen to constructive feedback and adapt as necessary, but never change who you are because of it. Your brand could be the next big thing, but you have to show the world your true self.

Secret #3: Find Your People

All six-figure businesses have a defined target audience. It's impossibly difficult to stand out in our oversaturated world without one.

As we discussed in chapter 1, total clarity around who your ideal customers are and why they need you is crucial to building a successful business. If there's only one major takeaway that sticks with you from this book, this is the one.

Focus on creating products, social media channels, descriptions, advertising, and a brand that appeals to one ideal customer base. Draw them in by speaking their language, understanding their wants and needs, and capturing their attention. Let everyone else go and focus on serving your people.

If you really nail this part, the right customers will always find you. You'll never have to worry about sales and your shop will experience automatic growth.

Secret #4: Try New Things

Six-figure business owners aren't afraid to innovate. You should always strive to try new things in your business.

Doing the same thing you've always done leads to the same results you've always gotten. If you want to skyrocket your business to new heights, you need to consistently transform and innovate.

This means adding new products to your store, trying out new tools for your business, testing out different keywords or email subject lines, and more.

A few guidelines here:

- Never drastically change what's already working well for you. As the saying goes, if it ain't broke, don't fix it.
- Don't make random changes to your business just for the heck of it. Make smart, deliberate, and measured changes only when it makes sense to.
- Whenever you try something new, keep a close eye on it and take note of its effects on your business. Some changes will drastically improve your shop, while others can detract from it. Allow new changes 30–90 days to collect data before fully evaluating them.

- Every business is different, so trying out new things for yourself is the only way to truly know what works best. This is how you'll grow. As you understand more about your customers, brand, and business model, you'll learn to do more of what works and less of what doesn't. You'll never know unless you try.

Secret #5: Avoid Burnout

As a small business owner, it's incredibly important to avoid burnout. Your business depends on you for growth, success, and income.

As the saying goes, you can't pour from an empty cup. You need to take care of yourself first, if you want your business to thrive.

When you're self-employed, it can be really tempting to work 16-hour days, just because you can. That's how it started for us and it quickly led to overwhelm, burnout, and a stall in our growth.

The long workdays became unsustainable. We ended up going through a boom and bust cycle with our business, where we were either working a ton or barely working at all because we were exhausted.

Slow and steady wins the race. If you want a six-figure business, you need to work at it consistently. This means taking breaks, hiring help, and adding a passive income stream (more on this later). Just like any other job, you need vacation days, sick days, and personal days.

If you want to live the dream, you need to avoid the grind. It's important to find that balance between hustle and overwhelm.

Look at it this way:

Business owner A works 16-hour days for four months in an attempt to hit six figures by the end of the year. She rarely takes a day off, often skips meals, and hasn't been prioritizing sleep. Eventually, she burns out and has to take a month off from her shop, just to recover and get the rest of her life back on track. She goes through this cycle two more times before she finally gives up on her business before ever reaching six figures.

Business owner B works eight-hour days consistently. She works hard on her shop five days a week, but still reserves evenings and weekends for her family, friends, and relaxation time. She takes one week off over the summer to go to the beach and recharge. Each month, she sees her Etsy income steadily climbing and within eighteen months, she has reached the six-figure mark with zero burnout. At this point, she's hired a virtual assistant and two production partners, while also adding a passive income stream to her shop. Best of all, her income is continuing to grow exponentially every month with even less work on her part, leaving more time for family, vacations, and hobbies.

As seen in the example above, while some shop owners will work super long days in an attempt to reach six figures faster, they're more likely to burn out and never reach their goals at all. Don't be that person. More is not always better and patience is a virtue.

Even if you do reach six figures working 16-hour days, is that truly sustainable? Do you really want to live that way for the rest of your career? You know the answer to this.

In the following sections, we'll go through the most important ways to avoid burnout in more detail.

Outsource + Diversify

One of the best ways to avoid overwhelm is knowing when to outsource and diversify.

As discussed in the previous chapter, outsourcing entails hiring out certain tasks for your business, once you're ready and can afford to. In addition to hiring out tasks in your business, you can also consider hiring out other responsibilities you have, such as cooking or cleaning, if that makes sense for you. It's basically whatever you need to do in order to maintain a balanced and reasonable workload throughout all areas of your life.

Diversifying, on the other hand, is a way to sell more products and skyrocket your income without significantly increasing your workload or needing to hire help. You'll learn exactly how to do this in the next chapter.

Self-Care

As a business owner and human being, it's important to make time for self-care. We are not robots or machines. We have limited resources and if we don't take time to recharge our batteries, burnout is inevitable.

Self-care consists of taking care of yourself in a way that enhances your health and well-being. This could be reading a book, taking a walk, enjoying a cup of tea, giving yourself a facial, practicing a guided meditation, writing in a journal, getting a massage, or anything else that feels good to you.

Engage in self-care activities regularly to stave off overwhelm and keep yourself going strong.

Time Off

All businesses must allow time off for their employees. This is because constant work with no breaks is unsustainable and leads to inefficiency and burnout.

The smart and necessary practice of giving workers time away from their jobs has been shown to actually enhance productivity, which leads to better output in the long run.

As the owner, you're still an employee of your own business and deserve time off, just like anyone else. Be sure to schedule a reasonable amount of vacation and sick days for yourself each year. This will help your business thrive.

Just remember to set your Etsy shop to "Vacation Mode" when you're away. Go to Shop Manager -> Settings -> Options -> Vacation Mode to turn this feature on. When you're in Vacation Mode, shoppers can still find your listings, but the "Add to Cart" button will be grayed out.

Instead, if you want to allow orders when you're away, you can increase your handling time for the length of your vacation plus a few days to catch up afterward. Just be aware this will result in extra work when you return.

CHAPTER 17

Can You Say Free Money?

Imagine creating an item just once and being able to sell it a thousand times over without any additional work. This is the magic of passive income. On Etsy, you can skyrocket your income quickly by adding a specific passive income stream centered around selling digital products.

As we've discussed in previous chapters, this is called diversification. You're essentially adding a new type of product to your Etsy shop that complements the ones you already have. It's a smart way to add an extra income stream without increasing your workload. You'll continue to sell your handmade items, while selling a selection of digital products as well.

This kind of passive income feels like free money because you're putting in the work once and getting paid for it indefinitely. There are also no materials to buy, labor to pay for, or studio space to rent. It's essentially a free way to increase your income that just takes a little bit of your time and a graphic design platform, such as Canva.

The addition of a passive income stream to your Etsy shop is the secret sauce to a multiple six-figure business. Once you've mastered digital products, you just rinse and repeat by adding more of them to your shop until you've reached the income level that you'd like.

With handmade products, there's a limit to how many you can feasibly make, package, and sell at one time. Even if demand increases for a specific handmade item, you can only create so many at a time, even with hired help.

By contrast, an unlimited amount of customers can purchase and download the same digital item automatically, which allows you to meet increasing demand without lifting a finger.

Digital items require no materials, shipping, or overhead. Plus, they take very little time and effort to create compared to handmade items. Once the digital item is selling in your shop, it's basically like free money deposited into your bank account on autopilot leading to an exponentially greater income potential.

Even if you're used to selling physical items only, we strongly encourage you to add at least a few digital products to your shop. Once you start, you'll become addicted. This is truly the easiest and fastest way to scale to multiple six figures and beyond.

Here's a summary of the benefits you'll experience from selling digital items:

- *Low overhead cost* – no need for materials, shipping, or inventory
- *High profit margins* – no physical materials means that all of the sale price (minus Etsy fees) is pure profit
- *Automation* – orders are delivered automatically with no fulfillment needed on your part, making the process hands-off (aka passive)
- *Fast learning curve* – super easy to create with no specialized skills needed
- *Quick cash* – you can have a new digital product up and selling within one day

- *Diversification* – more types of products means more options for customers to choose from

So, now that we've gone through the why, let's jump into the how.

First off, what is a digital product? It's simply an item that exists in digital form. Instead of receiving a physical item that is shipped to them, a customer who purchases a digital item will download it straight to their computer, smartphone, or other device. This means instant access, which customers love.

There are countless digital products out there, such as e-books, online courses, software, and membership sites. While you're free to explore these, the goal of this chapter is quick and easy additional income for your business, so you can scale to six figures quickly.

To this purpose, we'll only be exploring one kind of digital product in this book: printables. This is because printables are quick and easy to make, while requiring little to no overhead.

A printable is basically just a digital product that the customer can print out and use. An e-book or course can take months to create, whereas a printable takes just a few hours.

Etsy LOVES printables! There are thousands of sellers who make their income on Etsy solely through digital products. Now, you can make extra money from them too.

Here are examples of printables you can sell on Etsy:

- Planner pages
- Stationary
- Invitations

- Meal planners
- Trackers (e.g., chores for kids, weight loss goals, etc.)
- Coloring pages
- Journal pages
- Checklists
- Games (e.g., scavenger hunts, baby shower games, etc.)
- Worksheets
- Templates
- Flash cards

Choose digital products for your shop that your ideal customer would be interested in. These digital items should align with and complement the physical, handmade items you're already selling in your shop.

For example, if you sell baby items, such as baby blankets, nursery decor, and stuffed animals, your printables should match that same theme and customer base.

With this in mind, you could sell a baby essentials checklist, a new mom planner, or a baby shower game. These digital items would appeal to the same audience as your physical items, so your shop won't appear disjointed and sales will come in automatically.

To find the best printables to create for your niche, think about what customers searching for your best-selling items might also be looking for. For example, a customer searching for a wedding cake topper will likely also be interested in a printable wedding planner. You can also search the Etsy marketplace for inspiration using your niche or item name plus the word "printable" (i.e., wedding printable).

You should also ask for feedback from your Facebook Group and/or email list. Think about what your ideal customer needs and how you can provide it to them in digital form.

You can sell a single one-page printable or a pack of printables. A single printable will generally be priced between $0.99 and $1.99, while a pack of printables can range from $2.99 to $19.99 or more depending on how many pages it has. With no overhead, the sales price is pure profit after Etsy fees are deducted.

While this might not sound like big money, income from printables is made in volume. Remember that you only have to make the printable once and can then sell it indefinitely, making you money on autopilot. It's a bit of a time investment to create printables in the beginning, but once they're up and selling, it's basically free money.

We recommend Canva for creating printables. Canva has both a free and paid version available. You can try using the free one at first but may find yourself needing more features. At the time of this writing, Canva Pro costs just $119.99 per year, which is very little overhead compared to the crafting and shipping materials needed for physical products. It's well worth the investment and once you've made enough from digital items to cover the cost of Canva, the rest is pure profit.

In fact, if you've been following the steps in this book, you may even already have access to Canva or another graphic design platform for creating your logo, banners, and Pinterest Pins. Since you're likely already using Canva for other purposes, it costs NO additional money to use it to create printables as well. It's simply more bang for your buck.

There's a bit of a learning curve with creating printables, but with practice, it becomes easy. Canva is very intuitive and is specifically designed to help those with little to no graphic design experience create beautiful designs in minutes.

There are lots of articles and online tutorials out there that will teach you step by step how to create printables using Canva. Simply search the type of printable you're looking to create and the words "in Canva" on Google (e.g., how to create planner pages in Canva).

In addition to Canva, you can create printables using PicMonkey, Adobe Illustrator, or any other graphic design platform. Feel free to use what you already have or what feels easiest to you.

Remember that income made with digital products comes largely from volume. As you add more digital products to your shop over time, your profits will grow. Then, you can simply rinse and repeat until you've reached your desired income level.

As you continue to grow your shop, sales from your digital products will increase alongside your physical product sales. That's the whole point of diversification. It gives customers more options to choose from and increases the likelihood that they will make a purchase.

Digital products also widen your customer base. A customer may join your Facebook Group and email list after purchasing a printable for $1.99 and then go on to purchase over $100 worth of products from your shop later on.

All the elements of your shop work together in this way resulting in increased sales and income for your business over time. If you follow all the steps in this book, they will enhance and build upon each other to create a sustainable business with a consistent rise in sales. This is how you reach the six-figure mark and beyond.

Bonus Tip

Before we end this section, we wanted to share a special bonus tip for making extra income from your shop: gift wrapping.

A large percentage of customers on Etsy are shopping for gifts. In fact, 62% of US Etsy buyers reported that they were likely to buy gifts on Etsy during the 2021 holiday season. For this reason alone, gift wrapping is a popular service on Etsy, especially during the holidays.

This means you can make extra income for your shop, while also providing your customers with a convenient service that saves them time. Many people hate wrapping presents and are more than happy to pay a few extra dollars to have their item delivered all wrapped up and ready to go.

You can offer gift wrapping in your shop by going to Shop Manager -> Settings -> Options and then scrolling down to "Offer gift wrapping." Here, you'll set the price, details, and upload a preview photo. Once its enabled, gift wrapping options will appear on every listing, except for digital ones.

The items can either be traditionally wrapped or packaged in gift bags with tissue paper (this second option is a lot quicker unless you're a gift wrapping whiz!). Regardless of which one you choose, just make sure you indicate the type, color, and style of gift wrap you're offering in the details and preview photo, so customers know exactly what they're getting.

The price of gift wrapping on Etsy is $1 to $5 per order. To determine the best pricing for your shop, you should calculate the cost of your gift wrapping materials (wrapping paper, gift bags, tissue paper, bows, tape, etc.) and then charge three to four times that amount for the service. Buy your gift wrapping materials wholesale to increase your profit margins.

If you spend $1.23 per item for gift wrapping materials and you charge the customer $5, that's more than four times the cost of materials. For every item that's gift wrapped, you'll earn an additional $3.77 on top of the profit on the item itself. Even after subtracting Etsy fees, that's still an amazing profit margin that really adds up over time.

While gift wrapping isn't quite as passive as digital products, using gift bags instead of wrapping paper makes the process quick and easy. If done correctly, you shouldn't be spending much more time on gift wrapping than you would on regular packaging. Just make sure your gift wrapped items look beautiful and presentable.

CHAPTER 18

Keeping Up the Momentum

YOU DID IT! You now have an amazing Etsy shop that's both profitable and true to who you are. You've built a business that you can be proud of and are well on your way to earning the income of your dreams.

So, what's next? You keep going!

On this journey, you'll have amazing days and you'll have tough days. The key is to keep pushing forward, no matter what. If this is the dream, you'll need to have the drive to pursue it for the long haul.

This isn't a get-rich-quick scheme or an overnight sensation. This is about creating a sustainable business that you're passionate about that also provides a steadily growing income for you and your family.

It takes consistency, patience, and belief, but as long as you keep pushing each day, you'll get there!

In this chapter, we'll go through the three most important elements for keeping up momentum in your business.

Consistency

Consistency is the key to success. This may not be a sexy or revolutionary concept, but it works.

The path to a six-figure business is implementing the six steps outlined in this book consistently, day in and day out. Showing up each day and performing the tasks that move your business forward is how success happens.

Be sure to always treat your Etsy shop like a business and not a hobby, even if you're only working on it part-time. If you didn't show up to work for weeks on end with no explanation, you wouldn't expect your boss to still pay you, right? Your Etsy shop works the same way.

This is a marathon, not a sprint. Every step you take adds up over time. A six-figure business doesn't happen overnight, but if you stick with it and move forward a little bit each day, you'll start to see your dreams taking shape.

Patience

Patience is a virtue. You've heard it a hundred times before, but it still rings true.

While the blueprint we've laid out in this book is the quickest route to a six-figure Etsy shop, building a business inevitably takes time. You need to have the patience and drive to stick to it.

In our experience, it's always the people who ask, "How quickly can I reach $100,000 with my shop?" that end up quitting the soonest. They get discouraged when it doesn't happen overnight and move on to the next shiny new business idea that catches their attention. A year later, they're still spinning their wheels having made little to no progress on their goals.

Meanwhile, those who have stuck with their Etsy shop through the whole year are seeing real momentum and growth. This drives them to keep going.

The most successful Etsy business owners are the ones who have stuck with it the longest. It's that simple.

Keep this in mind and let your business grow in its own time. Whether it takes six months or two years to reach six figures, it's well worth the effort to build a business that's yours.

Belief

You need to believe in your dreams in order to make them happen. And more importantly, you need to believe in yourself.

It might sound cheesy, but the reality is, if you don't truly believe that you can build a six-figure Etsy shop, it'll be that much more difficult to stick with it for the long haul.

Just like any other business, your Etsy shop will experience many wins alongside occasional losses. In order to stick with it when the going gets tough, you need to believe deep in your heart that you are worthy of a six-figure business. This will give you the drive to push forward, no matter what.

As a final reminder, the most successful Etsy business owners are the ones who have stuck with it the longest. Be the one to maintain consistency, patience, and belief and you will WIN.

You Can Do This!

This book may be coming to a close, but your Etsy journey is just beginning! We're so happy for you and can't wait to see all that you'll accomplish.

You can do this. No matter who you are or where you come from or what struggles you've had in your past, if you want a successful Etsy business, you can have one. It just takes hard work, dedication, and believing that you can.

There's a lot of information in this book, so just take it step by step. Read through the book a second time and come up with a list of action steps.

Remember to complete the steps in order and resist the urge to jump around. Start with a strong foundation and keep moving forward each day. You'll get there.

We wish you all the success in the world. Thanks for being here and good luck!

Ready to build your Etsy empire? For a fully clickable list of all the tools, materials, and resources mentioned in this book, go to boundlessbooks.ck.page/etsy and sign up!
We'll deliver the list straight to your inbox.

Endnote

If you enjoyed this book, would you mind leaving us a quick review on Amazon? Each review means the world to us and helps us bring more books to you.

You can leave a review by searching for the book title on Amazon.com, scrolling to "Customer Reviews" at the bottom of the page, and clicking "Write a customer review" to the left of the screen.

Thanks again for reading!

References

Adams, R.L. (2016). The Three Fundamental Principles of Online Marketing. Retrieved from https://www.forbes.com/sites/robertadams/2016/04/04/the-3-fundamental-principles-of-online-marketing/?sh=3230f4062844

Cucu, E. (2021). [What Data Says] Where to Place Links in Facebook Posts for Greater Engagement. Here's what 51,054,216 Facebook Posts Tell Us. Retrieved from https://www.socialinsider.io/blog/link-in-facebook-comment/

Eaton, A. (2022). The Best Sizing for Etsy Product Photos [Updated April 2022]. Retrieved from https://www.amytakespictures.com/the-best-sizing-for-etsy-product-photos/

Etsy Staff. (2023). Etsy Help Center. Retrieved from https://help.etsy.com/hc/en-us?segment=selling

Etsy Staff. (2023). Etsy Seller Handbook. Retrieved from https://www.etsy.com/seller-handbook

Etsy Staff. (2021). Etsy Shopper Stats: November 2021. Retrieved from https://www.etsy.com/seller-handbook/article/etsy-shopper-stats-november-2021/1060970177431

Forsey, C. (2022). What is Marketing, And What's Its Purpose? Retrieved from https://blog.hubspot.com/marketing/what-is-marketing

Martin, M. (2022). 39 Facebook Stats That Matter to Marketers in 2023. Retrieved from https://blog.hootsuite.com/facebook-statistics/

Pasquali, M. (2022). Etsy: Number of Active Buyers 2012–2021. Retrieved from https://www.statista.com/statistics/409375/etsy-active-buyers/

TRUiC Team. (2022). Do I Need An LLC for my Etsy Entrepreneur Business? Retrieved from https://howtostartanllc.com/should-i-start-an-llc/etsy

Tsang, S. (2020). Best Mission Statements: 12 Examples You Need to See. Retrieved from https://www.fond.co/blog/best-mission-statements/

About the Authors

Alyssa and Garrett are married entrepreneurs with almost a decade of experience in the online business space. They've dabbled in everything from blogging and e-commerce to publishing and real estate.

Over the years, they've discovered a practical and reproducible framework for building highly profitable businesses in a short amount of time. Now, their passion lies in teaching budding entrepreneurs how to escape the grind and find financial freedom doing what they love.

When they're not building their entrepreneurial empire, Alyssa and Garrett enjoy travel, ballroom dancing, and Broadway shows.

Thanks for reading!